W9-AWH-652

Men-at-Arms • 352

The United States Army 1783–1811

James Kochan • Illustrated by David Rickman

Series editor Martin Windrow

First published in Great Britain in 2001 by Osprey Publishing,
Midland House, West Way, Botley, Oxford OX2 0PH, UK
44-02 23rd St, Suite 219, Long Island City, NY 11101, USA
E-mail: info@ospreypublishing.com

© 2001 Osprey Publishing Ltd.

All rights reserved. Apart from any fair dealing for the purpose of private study, research,
criticism or review, as permitted under the Copyright, Designs and Patents Act, 1988,
no part of this publication may be reproduced, stored in a retrieval system, or transmitted
in any form or by any means, electronic, electrical, chemical, mechanical, optical,
photocopying, recording or otherwise, without the prior written permission of the
copyright owner. Enquiries should be addressed to the Publishers.

Transferred to digital print on demand 2009

First published 2001
1st impression 2001

Printed and bound by PrintonDemand-Worldwide.com, Peterborough, UK

A CIP catalog record for this book is available from the British Library

ISBN: 978 1 84176 087 2

Editor: Martin Windrow
Design by Alan Hamp
Index by Alan Rutter
Originated by Colourpath, London, UK

Dedication

To my parents, Jakub and Georgene Kochan, for their love and encouragement, as well as their patience and guidance during
childhood family vacations that always included visits to a myriad of museums, historic sites, forts and battlefields.

Acknowlegements

Special thanks from both artist and author to Travis Crowder, Chuck Fithian, and John Livingston for their kind assistance during the
preparation of the color plates. I have benefitted from the generosity of persons too numerous to name, both institutional staff and
individuals, during my research on this subject over many years, but I would be remiss not to single out a few of the most helpful: Alan
Aimone, Brian Dunnigan, the late Detmar Finke, Bill Guthman, Peter Harrington, the late H.Charles McBarron, Ellen Miles, Dave
Simmons, John Steinle, Don Troiani, and lastly Marko Zlatich (who relocated the missing 'Hamilton drawings' – reproduced for the first
time in this work). It was a distinct pleasure to work again with historical artist and friend David Rickman; and we both extend our deep
and heartfelt thanks to editor Martin Windrow, ever patient, helpful and good-humoured.

Artist's Note

Readers may care to note that the original paintings from which the color plates in this book were prepared are available for private
sale. All reproduction copyright whatsoever is retained by the Publishers. All enquiries should be addressed to:

David Rickman, 1000 North Monroe Street, Wilmington, Delaware 19801, USA
E-mail: rickraak@sprintmail.com

The Publishers regret that they can enter into no correspondence upon this matter.

FOR A CATALOG OF ALL BOOKS PUBLISHED BY OSPREY
MILITARY AND AVIATION PLEASE CONTACT:

Osprey Direct, c/o Random House Distribution Center,
400 Hahn Road, Westminster, MD 21157
Email: uscustomerservice@ospreypublishing.com

Osprey Direct, The Book Service Ltd, Distribution Centre,
Colchester Road, Frating Green, Colchester, Essex, CO7 7DW
E-mail: customerservice@ospreypublishing.com

www.ospreypublishing.com

THE UNITED STATES ARMY 1783–1811

CHRONOLOGY

THE COMPLEXITIES of the organisation of the troops of the newborn United States in the decades immediately following the War for Independence are perhaps best listed for clarity in the following chronological notes:

April 1783 Declaration of the cessation of hostilities with Great Britain.

2 June 1784 Congress disbands the 700 troops remaining from the wartime Continental Army, with the exception of just 80 men: one 55-man artillery company at West Point, and a 25-man detachment at Fort Pitt.

3 June 1784 Congress passes resolution to raise a new force of 700 troops to be enlisted for one year's service, to be organised into eight companies of infantry and two of artillery, for the defense of the 'north western frontiers'. The troops are to be raised by quotas recommended to four states: Pennsylvania, New York, New Jersey and Connecticut. These troops are formed into the 'First American Regiment' under LtCol Josiah Harmar.

12 April 1785 The Congress of the Confederation of United States passes a resolution to raise troops for three years, most of the original 1784 enlistments having expired.

20 October 1786 In response to frontier unrest and a local agrarian revolt in western Massachusetts, Congress approves the augmentation of the original 700 troops to 2,040 men, plus officers, the whole to be formed as a 'Legionary Corps' to consist of:

1 battalion of artillery of 4 companies
2 troops of dragoons
1 battalion of rifle troops of 4 companies
3 regiments of infantry, each of 8 companies

30 January 1787 The War Department issues a circular describing the organisation and uniforms for the new Legionary Corps. In the event this force fails to materialise (with the exception of the artillery battalion, which is created from the two existing companies and two newly raised ones, under a major commandant), due to inadequate state support and the end of 'Shay's Rebellion'. The new recruits are absorbed into the First American Regiment under Harmar.

13 July 1787 The Northwest Ordinance is passed, creating government and settlement policies for the new Northwest Territory. The resulting influx of new American settlements increases tension with Indians within the Ohio River–Great Lakes region, and depredations mount on both sides during subsequent years.

LtCol Josiah Harmar was an excellent officer and a capable administrator, though inexperienced in frontier warfare; he is too often denied the credit which he is due for his role in organising and commanding the infant US Army. This undated miniature by Raphaelle Peale shows him in a blue coat faced buff, which he may have worn after being brevetted brigadier-general in 1787 – although it could also depict his dress as adjutant-general of the Pennsylvania militia, a position he held after resigning from the regular army on 1 January 1792. (Courtesy Diplomatic Reception Rooms, US Dept of State)

Capt John Pratt was commissioned in 1791 and served in the 1st Infantry (subsequently the 1st Sub Legion) until December 1793. He spent most of his time in the east, where he oversaw recruiting and supply matters and – as is evident in this 1792 portrait by Ralph Earl – did not encounter the shortages of food and clothing which plagued the troops on the frontier. His uniform conforms to 1787 regulations, though the collar is of the 'rise and fall' form rather than the simple standing collar specified. The scarlet lapels are unbuttoned, and his badge of the Society of the Cincinnati – indicating his prior service as an officer in the Continental Army – is proudly worn on the left lapel. The single silver epaulette on his right shoulder indicates his rank. In one hand he holds a short silver- or steel-mounted saber; in the other, a 1791 inspection return of the regiment. The 'sprangwork' sash of crimson silk, whose weave gave it elastic properties, is secured at top center to a vest button – perhaps an affectation, but more likely a necessary measure to prevent it slipping below his pronounced stomach. (Courtesy Dallas Museum of Art)

29 September 1789 Under the new Constitutional government, Congress passes an act to recognise the military establishment previously founded, consisting of 700 troops originally raised for service on the frontier, plus the additional two companies of artillery raised under the resolve of 20 October 1786.

30 April 1790 Congress passes an act to regulate and establish (in lieu of the former act) the military forces of the United States, to consist of:
1 battalion of artillery (of 4 companies)
1 regiment of infantry (of 3 battalions, each of 12 companies).

Fall 1790 Expedition consisting of 353 regular troops and 1,133 Kentucky and Pennsylvania militia under Harmar mount offensive against Miami Indian towns. Two advanced detachments are defeated on 19 and 21 October with nearly 200 regulars and militia killed

3 March 1791 Congress authorises an additional regiment of infantry, to be organised as the preceding one. The president is empowered to raise in addition to or in place of the militia, six-month troops enlisted under the denomination of 'Levies', not to exceed 2,000 rank and file.

Summer 1791 Two raids along the Wabash River are conducted by Kentucky mounted militia with partial success, destroying Indian towns and crops.

3 November 1791 A force of 1,400 regulars, levies and militia under MajGen Arthur St Clair, governor of the Northwest Territory, is routed in an attack on their camp on the eastern branch of the Wabash River (in present-day western Ohio) by Indians numbering between 1,000 and 1,500. In what has become known as 'St Clair's Defeat' more than 600 officers and men are killed and some 300 wounded – relative to the size of the force, the greatest defeat suffered by the US Army in its history.

5 March 1792 Congress passes an act to raise 'at the discretion of the president', for three years:
1 squadron of dragoons (of 4 troops)
3 regiments of infantry in addition to the two in service (each of 960 rank and file and organised in 3 battalions)

Another robustly built officer – LtCol William Darke, who commanded a battalion of Levies raised from the Virginia militia during the disastrous 1791 campaign. In this painting by Frederick Kemmelmeyer his uniform is cut in the style of the day, although the scarlet-faced blue coat has a fall-down collar rather than the more fashionable standing or rise-and-fall forms. Note the silver or white edging to his facings, the two silver epaulettes indicating field rank, and the silver plate on the white swordbelt; he carries a saber and a dirk. In the background troops with fixed bayonets are shown charging Indians; Darke led three such charges, all ineffective, during St Clair's defeat, yet miraculously survived with only a slight wound. The soldiers – dressed in blue coatees with red facings, white vests, brown linen overalls, round hats, and 'belly boxes' – almost certainly represent his Levies. (Courtesy The Museum of Early Southern Decorative Arts)

27 December 1792 The president directs the reorganisation of the military establishment (as allowed by the act of 5 March 1792) into the 'Legion of the United States', under the command of MajGen Anthony Wayne. The Legion is to be formed into 4 Sub Legions, each consisting of:
3 battalions of infantry (of 4 companies)
1 battalion of rifle troops (of 4 companies)
1 troop of dragoons
1 company of artillery
9 May 1794 Congress passes an act to organise a 'Corps of Artillerists and Engineers' to be incorporated with the artillery already in service, to be formed in 4 battalions of 10 companies each.
30 June 1794 Following the successful ambush of a supply train, some 1,500 Indians engage the relief force sent from nearby Fort Recovery and then attack the post, but are fought off by the garrison of Legion regulars.
20 August 1794 After advancing against the Miami villages on the Maumee River, Wayne and 1,000 Legion troops and Kentucky mounted volunteers defeat an Indian force of approximately 1,000 (including some 100 Canadian volunteers disguised as Indians) at the battle of Fallen Timbers, breaking the strength of the allied tribes.
3 August 1795 The Treaty of Greenville is signed with the Indians, who cede most of the lands that comprise present-day Ohio and eastern Indiana.
31 October 1796 The military establishment of the United States is reduced to:
The corps of artillerists and engineers
2 troops of light dragoons, to serve on horse or foot
4 regiments of infantry (each of 8 companies)
27 April 1797 Congress passes an act to provide for an additional (2nd) regiment of artillerists and engineers of 3 battalions, each with 2 companies.

16 July 1798 In the opening days of the 'Quasi-War' with France, Congress passes an act to augment the army by raising:
12 additional regiments of infantry (giving a total of 16)
1 regiment of dragoons (2 of its 8 troops already in service)

14 May 1800 The threat of possible war or invasion having passed, Congress discharges all officers and men raised under the acts to augment the army, except:
2 regiments of artillerists and engineers
2 troops of dragoons
4 regiments of infantry

16 March 1802 Congress fixes the Military Peace Establishment of the USA to consist of:
1 regiment of artillery of 5 battalions (each of 4 companies)
2 regiments of infantry (each of 10 companies)
A corps of engineers (not to exceed 20 officers and cadets)
A military academy, to be supervised by the chief engineer

28 February 1803 Congress authorises additional teaching staff for the academy, and 1 artificer and 18 enlisted men for the Corps of Engineers.

1803–1806 The Province of Louisiana is officially ceded to the USA by France (who had only received it from Spain three weeks earlier) on 20 December 1803, in the wake of the Louisiana Purchase. US regular forces begin to establish new military posts along the Mississippi River valley. Parties largely drawn from US Army personnel explore the vast new western territories. Tensions with Spain are exacerbated a 'filibustering' expeditions largely recruited and mounted from the US threaten the Spanish borderlands and Mexico.

12 April 1808 In the aftermath of the *'Chesapeake-Leopard* Affair' and in anticipation of war with Great Britain, a Congressional act is passed to raise, in addition to those corps then in service:
1 regiment of light artillery (of 10 companies)

While Wayne and his Legion mounted their campaign against the Ohio Indians in 1794, President Washington called out a volunteer army from the militia to suppress the 'Whiskey Insurrection' in western Pennsylvania – an agrarian revolt against the Federal excise tax on locally produced liquor. Many of the volunteers were armed, equipped and even uniformed by the Federal government. Washington's review of the Virginia and Maryland wing of the army at Fort Cumberland on 2 October 1794 is depicted here by Frederick Kemmelmeyer. (Courtesy, Winterthur Museum)

1 regiment of light dragoons (of 8 troops)
1 regiment of riflemen (of 10 companies)
5 additional regiments of infantry (each of 10 companies)

7 November 1811 At the battle of Tippecanoe, Governor William Henry Harrison and his army (consisting of the 4th US Infantry, Indiana militia and Kentucky volunteers) are surprised in their encampment by an early-morning attack by Indians under The Prophet, but succeed in salvaging a victory from near-defeat. This breaks the power of the confederated Indian tribes in the Northwest Territory.

UNIFORMS: THE FRONTIER CONSTABULARY FORCE, 1784–91

During 1784–85 the handful of regular troops left in the service of the United States were clothed in the same type of uniforms that they had previously worn in the Continental Army at the close of the War for Independence. It had been directed, by General Orders of 6 December 1782, that 'the Uniform of the American Cavalry and Infantry shall in future be, blue ground, with red facings and white linings and buttons', while the artillery would 'retain its present uniform' (blue with scarlet or red facings and linings and yellow trimmings). This initial attempt to provide a consistent uniform dress of blue with scarlet or red facings for United States troops would be followed in practice, to a large degree, until the War of 1812.

In May 1783, during the waning months of the war and in anticipation of the impending treaty with Great Britain, Gen George Washington directed Gen Henry Knox to provide the Continental Congress with cost estimates for troops intended to be raised (or kept in service) to occupy the frontier posts of the new nation. Included in the resulting estimates was a statement of the necessary articles of uniform dress with component breakdowns and their associated costs. This

Detail from the Kemmelmeyer painting of the Fort Cumberland review. Despite the naive execution of the background figures, the volunteers' blue coatees with red facings, white vests and overalls closely resemble those worn by regular infantry, and may have been provided from surplus Legion stocks; note the round hats and the use of belly boxes. The officers wear full-skirted coats and cocked hats, while the 'music' are in coatees of reversed colors. (Courtesy, Winterthur Museum)

remained of white wool cloth, as did the winter breeches and overalls (one pair of each being furnished annually, along with two pairs of linen overalls for hot weather). Meanwhile, the majority of the troops were now serving in the Ohio Valley and in the process of constructing and/or repairing frontier fortifications and barracks – demanding and arduous labor which would have worn out better quality clothing than that provided by contract. The surplus hunting shirts issued in 1784–85 had long ago been used up for fatigue duties, and during 1786–87 many troops labored 'under the disadvantage of having never received fatigue coats to save their long ones'. Some company commanders requested and received permission to 'have the coats...cut short' in order to use the excess cloth from the skirts to mend the coats, which would have to last their men until the next annual issue.

As it had been for generations before independence from Great Britain, fashionable dress in the infant United States was largely 'in the English taste', with some additional stylistic influence from recent ally France. Military uniforms were similarly cut along the lines of those furnished in the British Army, although much plainer as befitting 'republican tastes' (and near-empty military coffers), while rank insignia were more in keeping with the French system. On 30 January 1787 the War Office published a circular specifying the organisational structure and uniform regulations for the new 'legionary corps' of the United States. Although this expansion and reorganisation of the American military was only realised in small part, the infantry and artillery uniform specifications described therein appear to have been those employed

Although rather crude, this caricature or 'doodle' of an unknown officer from a Legion orderly book faithfully records the details of Legionary dress c.1794. His coatee has a standing collar decorated with a button each side, narrow lapels, and short skirts with diagonal 'slashed' pocket flaps. The epaulette on his shoulder is of the older 'rose knot' form – perhaps left over from his service during the Revolution? – rather than the simple strap style seen in most extant military portraits of this period. His hair is worn 'clubbed'; at left can be seen what appears to be a cocked hat (or perhaps a round hat with the left brim cocked up), with a circular cockade surmounted by a feather plume. (Courtesy The Filson Club)

Anthony Wayne wore this general officer's coat while commanding the US Legion and for his 1796 portrait by Elouis (see page 9). Of blue cloth with buff facings, it has the rise-and-fall collar popular until c.1798. Each functional lapel is finished with nine gilt buttons with 'worked' holes; the narrow cuffs each have three large buttons placed crosswise, while a smaller button closes the slit in the underseam. On the hips are pocket flaps edged with buff and bearing three 'blind' buttonholes, corresponding with the large buttons placed below. The coat skirts, lined with buff serge, are cut to come to the back of the knee. (Courtesy Historic Waynesborough; photographs John Steinle)

when contracting for army clothing during that and subsequent years, and are extracted below:

Hats cocked, and white trimmings [for infantry, yellow for artillery] – Coats blue, long and reaching to the knee, scarlet lapells, cuffs and standing cape, white buttons and linings [for infantry, with yellow buttons and scarlet linings for artillery]....

Vests of the Artillery and Infantry to be white, yellow buttons for the artillery and white for the infantry, short flaps, three buttons on each pocket.

Overalls – to all species of troops....

Lapells of the whole, and standing capes, two inches wide, cuffs three inches [deep].

Stocks – all the troops to wear black stocks or cravats.

Cockades – Infantry and Artillery, black leather, round, with points, four inches in diameter.

Shoulder straps – all the troops to have blue, edged with red on both shoulders.

The uniform of the musicians to be red, faced with blue.

From reading the above, there appears to have been but little change in the dress from that previously issued, although for the first time we find the mention of 'standing capes' (collars) rather than the flat or fall-down collar as used in both the British and American military during the War for Independence and beyond. Although some fashion-conscious British colonels had furnished their regiments with coats having standing collars as early as 1782, this was in contravention to the clothing warrant of 1768; it would not be until 1796 that the new form of collar officially received Crown sanction. Thus, in at least one respect, the United States Army were ahead of their British counterparts.

Harmar was not happy with the blue woollen overalls and the hats provided that year, and reiterated his view in early 1788 that the uniform should always consist of long blue coats faced with red, white smallclothes and cocked hats. Knox

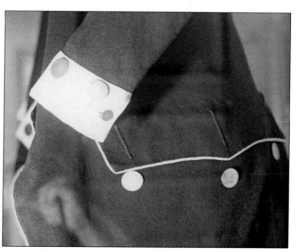

Capt Griffith John McRee, who served in the Corps of Artillerists and Engineers 1794–98, painted in 1795 by James Peale. His blue uniform, faced scarlet, is trimmed with gilt buttons, and a gold 'strap' epaulette on his right shoulder as appropriate to his branch and grade. Note that the white vest has a standing collar while that on the coat is of rise-and-fall form. (Courtesy Mead Art Museum, Amherst College)

explained that the colored overalls were due to unavailability of white goods on the market, and that in future winter overalls would be of white 'if to be obtained'. However, he disagreed with Harmar's notions of proper military dress, noting that while 'Overalls are conceived to be preferable to breeches' for legwear, short coats were preferable to long 'for the service of the frontiers', and 'long coats and cocked hats are in my opinion an unseemly association'. Knox closed the discussion with the following paragraph:

'It has been my desire that the American troops should have a characteristically national uniform, blending utility and appearance without implicitly following the customs of the Europeans. I have had the hope that something might be adopted in this respect, might evince a judgement of our own, although I confess that the present uniform is very different from my wishes and judgement, yet long coats and cocked hats would not be parts of the uniform. I hope the time will arrive when a system of this kind may be adopted agreeable to troops and honorable to the nation.'

This insight would foretell some changes that Knox intended to implement in the not-too-distant future, as well as the quest for an ideal 'national uniform' that would continue to plague American military leaders for decades to come.

At Fort Harmar and other western posts of the 1st American Regiment, however, the lieutenant-colonel commandant did his best to bring about a uniform and martial appearance among his troops, despite sporadic issues of sometimes 'sleazy' articles of clothing. Although Harmar had hoped for hats with brims wide enough to be cocked up with the back fan higher than the front, the wool felt hats received were apparently narrow- and even-brimmed and scarcely able to be cocked at all. As detachments of recruits arrived from the east during 1788, Harmar ordered officers to have 'the White binding taken off their mens Hats', which were trimmed instead with bearskin crests and plumes made of red-dyed buck tails – both readily available from local resources. This headgear continued to be worn by the original 1st Regiment, and apparently by the newly raised 2nd Infantry in 1791, although a red feather replaced the buck tail plume in 1790.

The artillery and two regular infantry regiments were dressed very much as prescribed in the 1787 uniform regulations when they took the field in 1791, with the exception of the headgear noted above for the infantry regiments. However, the Federal government also had the responsibility of clothing and equipping the 1st and 2nd Regiments of Levies. Raised for only six months' service, these troops received a cheap uniform dress consisting of short blue coats or 'coatees' with vests and overalls. The coatees had red facings and lapels but these were probably 'false', i.e. incapable of buttoning across, instead being merely sewn down to the breast for decorative purposes. They were also apparently unlined or only partly lined, and made of coarse materials. The government realised substantial savings in cloth and labor, but the cheap uniforms subsequently wore out long before the enlistments of their wearers. The levies received wool felt round hats; it is doubtful that embellishments such as the bearskin crests and feathers used by the regulars (who paid for such through whiskey or pay stoppages) were ever applied.

THE LEGION OF THE UNITED STATES, 1792–96

Following St Clair's disastrous 1791 Indian campaign, Secretary of War Knox finally saw his plan for a 'Legion of the United States' come to fruition, and with his War Department subordinates he developed patterns and contracted for uniforms and equipment for the new model corps. Gone were the infantry's long coats and cocked hats so disliked by Knox, now replaced with coatees and round hats. Distinctive coatees with 'round skirts' (i.e. without turnbacks) had been developed for the newly raised light dragoons and rifle troops, further distinguished from line troops by red wings at the termination of their shoulder straps. In the meantime, at 'Legionville' (established 20 miles down the Ohio River from the taverns, stills and brothels of Pittsburgh), MajGen Anthony Wayne began to mold the new organisation from raw recruits and the surviving elements of the regular infantry and artillery.

While the new clothing was being prepared, Knox ordered Wayne on 27 July 1792 to provide 'distinctive marks' for the hats of the respective Sub Legion: white binding and plumes for the 1st, red for the 2nd, yellow for the 3rd, and unbound hats with black plumes for the 4th Sub Legion. However, writing to Knox on 13 September, Wayne requested binding for the headgear and confessed that he had 'taken the liberty to make some Addition to the distinctive marks of the four Sub Legions, to those you directed – particularly that of metamorphosing the heterogenous of Hats (for they had got out of shape or form) into Uniform Caps' – and enclosed a copy of his general order posted two days earlier:

The Officers being Arranged to the four Sub Legions, it now becomes expedient to give these Legions distinctive Marks, which are to be as follows – Viz

The first Sub Legion white Binding upon their Caps, with white plumes and Black hair.

The second Sub Legion – Red binding to their Caps, red plumes, with White hair.

The third Sub Legion – Yellow Binding to their Caps – Yellow plumes, and Black Hair.

The fourth Sub Legion – Green binding to their Caps – with Green Plumes and white hair.

Converting old, disfigured hats into uniform light infantry-type caps was a technique that Wayne had

Considered a superior cavalry officer, Solomon Van Rensselaer entered service as a cornet in 1792, was a captain the following year, and was senior major when discharged as a consequence of the army's reduction in June 1800. This miniature of c.1797 by Robert Field shows him in the pre-1799 light dragoon uniform worn during the Legion and early 'Quasi-War' periods. The blue coat is faced scarlet and trimmed with silver buttons and epaulette; note the scarlet wings on the shoulders, and the two small buttons on the rise-and-fall collar – details not mentioned in extant records. It is not surprising that dragoons adopted the wings originally specified for riflemen: both were employed as elite light troops. Van Rensselaer's black leather shoulder belt mounts an oval silver plate bearing an eagle device. (Courtesy The Albany Institute of History and Art)

successfully employed when commanding Pennsylvania troops during the War for Independence. The brim was trimmed off except for that in front, which remained to form a visor, and the parings were used to make small, vertical 'shields' or front plates. Although Wayne attempted to preserve the color distinctions prescribed by Knox for the first three Sub Legions, he had instituted green binding and plumes in lieu of plain black for the Fourth, probably to prevent any perception of a slight among its officers and men. Wayne ordered the officers to wear 'plain Cock'd Hatts with no other Distinctive marks, but the plumes of their respective Sub Legions, except in actual Service or action, when they will wear the same Caps' as worn by their men. Tails from slaughtered cattle were used to provide the hair, which was mounted to the caps in the form of the crest or 'comb'.

Wayne notified Knox on 10 August that 'the troops & Dragoons improve rapidly in Manoeuvre, but our coats begin to be out in the Elbows & under the Arms'; he requested 'remnants of blue cloth with Needles & thread, by which means we can furbish up & keep our Clothing decent & comfortable which will tend to inspire the troops with pride...'. More than a month elapsed before Knox promised that both the requested materials and colored binding would soon be forwarded, and these appear to have been received by early December.

As late as 30 December 1792 many of the caps were still not fully trimmed, and it was noted that 'Hair for the completion of the caps may be had upon proper returns'. However, this failure seems to have been due not so much to any deficiency of cow tails as to a dislike of both the cut-down headgear and the hair 'combs' among many of the officers and soldiery. On 9 May 1793, Wayne was 'astonished after the pointed and Repeated orders' concerning headgear and military appearance to find that Capt Uriah Springer had still not 'caused his hats to be cut and form'd into Caps', and placed the officer and his rifle company on fatigue duties until the 'Orders of Uniformity are fully accomplished'. Despite such admonitions and punishments, some companies (possibly ones that had just joined the main body of the Legion, now encamped above present-day Cincinnati, Ohio, at Hobson's Choice) had still not provided hair for the caps and were ordered to do it by the 16th of that month. Still later, on 16 October, we find Wayne forming fatigue parties 'compos'd of all such men from the... Infantry, light Infantry & Rifle men...who have lost or destroy'd the Comb from their Caps...'.

By 10 March 1794 'Mad Anthony' Wayne had finally given up on converting the hats to the unpopular caps, and while he still detested the 'inferior quality of the Hats' he seems to have fixed upon a solution very much like that introduced in 1788 by Harmar. The hats, 'which with the least wet, dropt over the ears & eyes of the men & entirely looses their form', he 'caused to be in some degree remedied by a strong binding & adding a bear skin cover in the form of a crest over the Crown which not only keeps the heads of the men dry & warm but has a Military & Martial Appearance'.

Thomas Cushing was major of the 1st Infantry when he sat in 1799 for this miniature by James Peale. His coat conforms to the infantry uniform regulations of 1787 and 1796, and he displays the Cincinnati eagle on its blue and white ribbon. His white vest is double-breasted, as ordered in January 1799 for all infantry officers serving under the command of BrigGen James Wilkinson. Both coat and vest have standing collars, the former with a silver button and worked hole on each side. (Courtesy Indianapolis Museum of Art, gift of Josiah K.Lilly Jr)

George Washington Parke Custis, the adopted son and step-grandson of George Washington, received a cornet's commission in the light dragoons in 1799. In accordance with the original 17 January uniform circular, which specified white facings and trimmings for the light dragoons, Washington procured silver-mounted arms and accoutrements, as well as a uniform, for his young ward. Painted in 1801 by Robert Field following his discharge as lieutenant during the army's 1800 reduction, Custis is shown here in a green coat with the black facings which had replaced the original white by October 1799. However, his epaulette, buttons and lace are still silver and the holes are placed in pairs, rather than of yellow metal and singly spaced as finalised for that corps by the close of the year. Clearly, Custis wore this uniform throughout his short service – an example of the various interpretations and uncertainties over army officers' dress that prevailed during the Quasi-War period and beyond. (Courtesy The Virginia Historical Society)

At the same time, Wayne proposed that in the forthcoming clothing issue the white woollen overalls then in use be replaced with ones of brown or blue cloth (which masked dirt and stains) and – as had Harmar before him – he requested long coats and cocked hats in preference to the coatees and 'flimsy round' hats introduced by Knox. He explained that 'long Coats will keep [the men] warm & comfortable during the Winter & be curtailing them in the spring, they will afford patches or materials for repairing or mending them when reduced to Coatees'. President Washington thought the 'ideas communicated ... [by Wayne relative] to long and short Coats are not, I conceive, bad'. Rumors abounded concerning a possible change in dress, and one infantry officer, writing to Samuel Hodgdon in late September, enquired about 'What Form the new Uniform will be' and assured the Superintendent of Military Stores that 'Should you Succeed In getting a Long Coat, and Cockt. Hatt the Whole Army will Feel themselves Under Obligations to You'.

However, there were sufficient stocks of coatees on hand to clothe most of the troops for at least another year, with the exception of the artillery, most of whom (especially the new-raised troops serving in the East) received long-skirted coats beginning in mid-1795. Although an artilleryman serving in the Northwest Territory wore a yellow-trimmed hat, things were different with his counterpart in the East. The new commandant of the 'Corps of Artillery', LtCol Stephen Rochefontaine, had apparently convinced Secretary of War Timothy Pickering to contract in mid-1795 for 'helmets (or Horsemans Caps)' with bearskin crests and red plumes for the new corps in lieu of hats, and these began issue late that year. 'Dam them I despise them they must look like the divel with long Coats', wrote Maj Henry Burbeck, who had commanded Wayne's field artillery – a sentiment apparently shared by fellow veteran artillerists; and there is little evidence of their use in the field or in frontier garrisons. An inventory of September 1797 reveals that the 282 artillery caps still on hand in Philadelphia were listed as 'now used for Cavalry' – providing at least some public benefit from an expensive experiment gone bad.

THE QUASI-WAR PERIOD, 1797–1800

In anticipation of new infantry coats with longer skirts, regulations were issued from headquarters on 12 February 1796 prescribing the new uniform for infantry officers, which was to consist of a blue coat 'reaching to the knee and full trimmed' with 2in-wide standing collar and lapels, 3in-wide cuffs, white metal buttons and trimmings, and worn with white smallclothes, black boots and cocked hats. On 19 January 1799, BrigGen Wilkinson further clarified the 'under cloathes' of the officers, which were to consist of 'half boots with white pantaloons & vests double breasted'. With the exception of a more modern cut, the uniform was essentially unchanged from that of the 1787 regulations.

It would not be until late 1797, however, that the enlisted infantrymen would finally receive their new pattern coats, and it is questionable whether the wait was worth it. It appears to have been a rather plain garment of blue, with scarlet facings consisting of standing collar, lapels with seven large pewter buttons, and cuffs that were slit on the under-seam and secured there with one small button and hole – their sole embellishment. It had been intended to trim the coats with narrow, white worsted binding and this appears to have been done during the first year, but with the creation of 12 additional infantry regiments in 1798 to supplement the four standing regiments, such time- and money-consuming niceties were soon discarded. The blue shoulder straps remained as they had been for years, edged with scarlet and secured at the junction of the collar and shoulder seam with a small button on each shoulder. Skirts were longer and capable of being hooked together to form turnbacks, exposing their linings of white shalloon or serge (the body of the coat was unlined). The outer pocket flaps found on the hips of most military coats during this period (generally non-functional) were deleted as an expensive superfluity, but functional pockets remained inside the skirts.

The vest and overalls were of the same patterns as worn during the Legion period, although one of the two pairs of winter overalls issued was now made of blue cloth or kersey. Another Legionary carryover was

RIGHT **Prepared at the behest of Inspector-General Alexander Hamilton during summer 1799, this drawing shows the uniform which was proposed, and later made up, for the enlisted men of the Regt of Light Dragoons. The coat is green (although the watercolor has now faded to a bluish shade), with black facings and yellow buttons; the sleeves and skirts are trimmed with herringbone holes of yellow 'ferret'. This drawing, and others prepared at the same time to accompany another proposed version of the 1799 regulations, constitute the earliest known schematics of US Army uniforms extant. (Courtesy Library of Congress)**

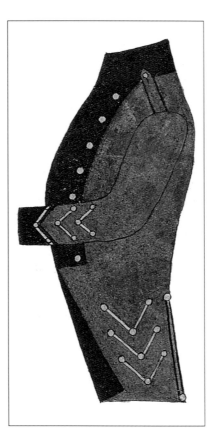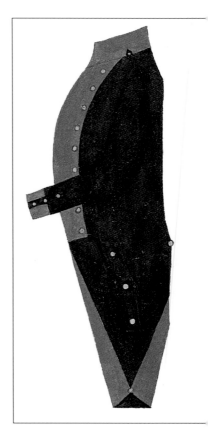

Modifications to the 9 January 1799 uniform 'regulation' were already under consideration when this 'broadside' was being printed, although some of its guidelines – particularly those concerning officers' dress and insignia – were at least partly implemented. (Courtesy Library of Congress)

OPPOSITE Schematic drawing of an artillery enlisted man's uniform prepared to accompany a proposed revision of the 1799 regulations. The coat is blue with red facings and linings and yellow buttons. Red-edged pocket flaps are set vertically on the skirts; the shoulder straps end in blue wings, and both are edged red. This uniform was actually made up and issued during 1799–1801, and continued in use, with the addition of yellow binding and a few other minor changes, for a number of years. (Courtesy Library of Congress)

UNIFORM *for the* ARMY *of the* UNITED STATES

THE uniform of the commander in chief, to be a blue coat, with yellow buttons, and gold epaulets, each having three silver stars, with lining, cape and cuffs, of buff—in winter buff vest and breeches;—in summer, a white vest and breeches of nankeen.—The coat to be without lappels, and embroidered on the cape and cuffs and pockets. A white plume in the hat, to be a further distinction. The Adjutant General, the aids, and secretaries, of the commander in chief, to be likewise distinguished by a white plume.

The uniform of the other general officers, to be a blue coat, with yellow buttons, gold epaulets, linings and facings of buff—the under-cloathes the same with those of the commander in chief.

The major generals, to be distinguished by two silver stars, in each epaulet, and except the inspector general, by a black and white plume, the black below——The brigadier to be distinguished, by one silver star on each epaulet, and by a red and white plume, the red below. The aids, of all general officers, who are taken from regiments, and the officers of inspection, to wear the uniforms of the regiments, from which they are taken. The aids to be severally distinguished by the like plumes, which are worn by the general officers, to whom they are respectively attached.

The uniform of the aids of the commander in chief, when not taken from regiments, to be a blue coat, with yellow buttons, and gold epaulet, buff lining and facings —the same under-cloathes with the commander in chief.

The Inspector general, his aids, and the officers of inspection generally, to be distinguished by a blue plume. The Quarter Master General, and other military officers in in his department, to be distinguished by a green plume.

The uniform of the infantry and artillery to be a blue coat, with white buttons, and red facings, white under-cloathes and cocked hats—the length of the officer's coats to reach to the knees, the coats of the infantry, to be lined with white, of the artillery with red. The uniform of the cavalry, to be a green coat, with white buttons lining and facings; white vest and breeches, and helmet caps.

Each Colonel, to be distinguished by two epaulets; each Major, by one epaulet on the right shoulder, and a strap on the left. All the Field Officers, (except as above) and the Regimental Staff, to wear red plumes—the Officers of Companies are to wear no plumes.

Captains to be distinguished by an epaulet on the right shoulder: Lieutenants by one on the left shoulder; Cadets, by a strap on the right shoulder. The epaulets and straps of the regimental officers to be of silver.

Serjeant-majors and Quarter-master-serjeants, to be distinguished by two red worsted epaulets; Serjeants by a like epaulet on the right shoulder; Corporals, by a like epaulet on the left shoulder; the flank companies to be distinguished by red wings on the shoulders.

The coats of the Musicians to be of the colours of the facings of the corps to which they severally belong. The Chief Musicians to wear two white worsted epaulets.

All the Civil Staff of the Army, to wear plain blue coats, with yellow buttons, and white under-cloathes.

No gold or silver lace, except in the epaulets and straps to be worn.

The commissioned officers, and cadets, to wear swords.

All persons belonging to the army, to wear a black cockade, with a small white Eagle in the centre. The cockade of non-commissioned officers, musicians and privates, to be of leather, with Eagles of tin.

The regiments to be distinguished from each other, numerically. The number of each regiment to be expressed on the buttons.

By Command of the President

GIVEN at the War Office of the United States, in Philadelphia, this 9th day of January, A. D. 1799, and in the twenty-third year of the Independence of the said states.

JAMES M'HENRY,

Secretary of War.

the round hat 'decorated with loops and bearskin', although the distinctive colored binding appears to have been discontinued with the dissolution of the sub legions in 1796. The hat was left rather plain, with only the white 'string' loopings that secured the tooled leather cockade to the cocked-up left brim providing some contrast to the black felt and fur crest.

As the United States prepared to plunge into war with the Revolutionary French government, its three senior military leaders – George Washington, who reluctantly came out of retirement to serve his country once again as newly appointed 'Commander of the Armies of the United States', and MajGens Charles Cotesworth Pinckney and Alexander Hamilton – met in Philadelphia during November and December 1798 to confer on important military matters. Among the topics of discussion were the uniforms, arms and equipment of the expanded army. Their initial recommendations, submitted to Secretary of War James McHenry (both McHenry and Hamilton had served as aides to Washington during the War for Independence) were published and circulated by the Secretary on 9 January 1799.

As the broadside (see page 17) reached the hands of new and veteran officers alike, it raised as many questions as it answered concerning the uniforms they and their men were to wear. Inundated with requests for additional details, McHenry tasked Hamilton to develop detailed specifications and patterns for the army's uniforms. In the interim, uniforms had already been contracted in 1798 for the 12 additional regiments as well as the veteran corps. They were all made to the 1797 pattern already in use, although one or two of the changes recommended in the printed order were implemented. To distinguish

BELOW LEFT **The 'frog-legged' or 'turkey' eagle form popular during the Federal period is very evident on this engraved silver belt plate worn between 1799 and 1801 by Lt Thomas Eastland of the 4th Infantry. (Private collection by family descent)**

BELOW **Another version of the eagle belt plate is known to have been worn by officers in some of the 'Additional' regiments raised in New England during 1799–1800; this example belonged to Erasmus Babbet of the 14th Infantry. (Courtesy J.Duncan Campbell; photograph Mike O'Donnell)**

Fevret St Memin must have executed this profile protrait of LtCol Henry Burbeck of the 1st Regt of Artillerists & Engineers before 1802, as his hair is still worn long; the buttons are also of a pattern used by both regiments of this corps from c.1799–1801. The collar has two buttons with gold-laced holes, while the lapels have holes of scarlet 'twist' – known features of artillery officers' uniforms during this period. (Courtesy National Portrait Gallery, Smithsonian Institution)

the infantry regiments from one another pewter buttons were struck with 'the number of each regiment ... expressed on the buttons', replacing the frog-legged eagle device formerly used.

Due to the sudden and massive demands in the marketplace for cloth suitable for military uniforms, supplies of suitable white and blue cloth or kersey for overalls were hard to come by in 1799 and, as a stop-gap, various other hues were accepted. Captain Shaumburg of the 2nd Infantry complained to his colonel that his company had been issued 'Woolen Overalls of all Colours imaginable and those of the worst kind', noting that it was 'the first instance to my Recollection that one Company has been Cloathed so Fantastically'. The stamped leather cockades were now to bear a small eagle in the center, originally ordered to be of 'tin' for all enlisted troops, but subsequently modified to include brass examples for the artillery to match the metal used in the plain artillery buttons (the first eagles produced were not delivered until mid-1799).

Hamilton and his subordinates continued their work on the uniform regulations throughout 1799, preparing and submitting at least two early drafts to the Secretary and a 'final' document on 19 December. Hamilton even had prototype uniforms made for the different branches and, at the prompting of the contractor for the new dragoon uniforms, forwarded the coat for his examination before it had received official approval from McHenry. The contractor, already behind schedule due to such governmental indecision, went ahead and had nearly completed all of the dragoon coats when McHenry vetoed the new uniform due to its expense. Thus the dragoons were the first to receive uniforms in accordance with one or more versions of the 1799 regulations floating about. Stocks of artillery uniforms were also depleted, and to clothe the expanded corps the go-ahead was given to make up new artillery coats as well. Before new uniforms could be prepared for the infantry the threat of war with France had waned, and the additional troops, including the 12 new infantry regiments, were disbanded in 1800.

The uniform that Hamilton proposed for the infantry included blue coats which extended to the knee and had scarlet facings with worked buttonholes, horizontal pocket flaps and full linings. Pantaloons of blue with red edging, or all-white ones for parade, would be worn inside black gaiters, while broad cocked hats completed the uniform. McHenry balked at the estimated costs: $8.50 per coat and $1.25 for the hat, as opposed to $4.50 and $.80 respectively for coats and hats 'under the Old form'. By late April 1800 McHenry, caught between a persuasive

LEFT **Honorably discharged from the army in June 1802 during the Jeffersonian purge of officers either foreign born or strongly Federalist in sympathy, LtCol Louis Tousard wears the fully laced uniform first specified for the artillery in April 1801. This St Memin engraving also shows him with cropped hair, further supporting a date of 1801–02. (Author's collection)**

BELOW **Adopted in 1779, Von Steuben's** *Blue Book* **governed the 'order and discipline' of the US Army until replaced during the War of 1812. This is a detail from a plate showing the 'manual exercise' prepared for the 1803 edition. Clearly visible are the new-pattern round hats and pantaloons with gaiters introduced during 1801–02, as well as the use of crossbelts and bayonet scabbards – a practice which had fallen from favor and was only at this time being gradually re-established. (Author's collection)**

Hamilton and an irate President John Adams, finally ordered the Military Store Keeper to 'produce the former pattern Garments, as those by which the Clothing now ordered are to be cut out'. With the reduction of the army no additional infantry uniforms were necessary, as sufficient were on hand for the old regiments; but by the time the contracts were countermanded the Purveyor of Public Supplies reported that at least most of the infantry 'Coats were all cut out & part of the other articles'.

In the meantime BrigGen James Wilkinson, who commanded the troops that had formerly comprised the Legion – now serving on the Great Lakes and along the Mississippi – had received a copy of Hamilton's proposed uniform regulation of December 1799. Believing it (or wishing it) finally approved, he published it in his general orders of 30 March 1800 and ordered 'all officers ... to conform accordingly'. At the War Department things were in an even more confused state. Hamilton had been discharged as Inspector General in June, and that same month, in a final break with Adams, McHenry resigned as Secretary of War. In September the new Inspector General wrote to the confused commander of the 2nd Infantry that:

'... *A change of white for yellow Buttons, Epaulets etc., was proposed during the lifetime of the twelve Regiments and the lace had been previously abolished by Mr.McHenry who published a scheme for the uniform of*

JEFFERSON'S REPUBLICAN ARMY, 1801–08

The promised general order had still not been issued when the Federalist administration was ousted by the Republicans. The new Secretary of War, Henry Dearborn, following the lead of President Thomas Jefferson, focused his immediate attention on purging as many Federalists from the armed forces as possible, and finally addressed the subject of uniforms on 17 April 1801. He forwarded a pattern infantry coat to the Purveyor, apparently one of those made up earlier to Hamilton's specifications. Winter overalls remained as before, one pair blue and one pair white, although now edged on the outseam with a welt of white or blue cloth respectively. The white summer overalls (also with blue edging) were made without 'tongues' or gaiter-bottoms, being designed instead to be worn inside blackened duck gaiters that buttoned with four (later nine) small buttons. The round hat's bearskin crest formed a pronounced arch over the flat-topped crown, created from 'wires' mounted to the bearskin. The hat was 'bound with strong white binding', the 'side of the hat not to be turned up as heretofore', while the cockade and eagle were mounted on the left near the top of the crown and surmounted by 'a Deer's tail plume, white'.

Artillery coats were ordered 'to be made as usual, with the addition of yellow trimmings where the Infantry Coats have white; the vests and heretofore; overalls or pantaloons similar to the Infantry, except the seams to be yellow in all cases; moderate sised cocked hats, with ... cockades, and red plumes ... bound with strong yellow binding...'. New pattern buttons of stamped yellow metal were to be made for the artillery, bearing the device of an eagle on a fieldpiece, while pewter infantry buttons were to be cast bearing an eagle with the number of the regiment. There still being significant stocks of the old pattern infantry and artillery overalls on hand, the Secretary still hoped that the Purveyor would endeavor to provide each soldier with at least one pair each of new pattern summer and winter overalls, the remainder of the soldier's annual allowance being completed with legwear of the old form during 1801–02.

The Purveyor, who feared the infantry uniforms would prove too expensive to make, appended the remarks of principal tailors, who thought the 'forepart is cut too rounding' and the 'Collar & Upper part of the Lappels [being] broader than the lower part or the Cuff ... [were] out of proportion'. They thought the lapels had too many buttons, 'set 8 on each side would look better than 10', while the three large buttons placed crosswise on each cuff should be made without buttonholes.

The coat worn by Jacob Kingsbury in this miniature conforms to that known to have been established for infantry officers by the second part of 1801. The cut generally follows the December 1799 'Hamilton' regulations, with the addition of laced buttonholes and edged facings. Kingsbury served as a major in the 3rd Infantry from 1797 until promoted lieutenant-colonel of the 1st Infantry in 1803, and the painting was probably done to commemorate his new rank. The Cincinnati eagle is still being worn on his left lapel. (Courtesy The National Society of the Cincinnati, Anderson House Museum)

Thomas Hunt succeeded to the colonelcy of the 1st Infantry in April 1803 on the death of John Hamtramck. He appears to have retained many of that former commander's standing orders concerning regimental dress, such as the use of this silver regimental gorget; it was suspended by a yellow ribbon in 1801, replaced by a red one in July 1802. This portrait was probably done shortly before Hunt's death in 1808, as the square-breasted lapelled coat does not seem to have been used by infantry officers much earlier than 1806. The practice of wearing the crimson officer's sash over the left shoulder, rather than around the waist per extant regimental orders, could be an unchronicled distinction or merely artistic licence. His gorget and sash obscure the oval silver plate mounted on the white shoulderbelt. (Private collection by family descent; author's photograph)

The dashing young Zebulon Pike had only recently been promoted to major in the newly raised 6th Infantry when he sat for this portrait by Charles Willson Peake in 1808. His epaulettes have red straps with silver fringe; whether this was a regimental distinction or a personal affectation is unknown, but this style has not been observed in any other portraits of US Army officers from this period. (Courtesy Independence National Historical Park)

Finally, he reminded the Secretary that there were still in store 1,200–1,500 ready-made infantry coats of the 1797 or 'old uniform', with more than 2,000 additional coats cut out and folded up in bundles with all necessary trimmings to complete them, less buttons. Rather than altering the old uniforms to conform to the new pattern with the attendant expenses, the Purveyor succeeded in convincing him to continue using the old pattern until all remaining stocks were depleted. Dearborn had wished to further modify the infantry and artillery coats to include buttonholes bound with narrow binding, and although this measure was postponed for the infantry it was fully implemented with the artillery coats, which in 1801 were modified to include false buttonholes of yellow tape.

With further reductions in the military establishment the following year, there were still sufficient coats and other clothing stocks on hand to provide for most of the army's needs until mid-1803, when the subject of new pattern uniforms was readdressed. Thus, during its first term, the anti-military Jefferson administration (which blocked implementation of many critical army reforms initiated by the previous Federalist administration, and claimed credit for others that ultimately survived – such as a Military Academy, a Federal arsenal a Harpers Ferry, and the introduction of horse artillery) was able to demonstrate significant budgetary savings and at the same time to clothe its depleted army in a comfortable manner To his credit, Dearborn (a former military man himself did have the interests of the troops in mind and approved the introduction of a number of small improvements to the dress of the soldiery beginning in 1802, with the issue of fatigue frocks and trousers to save their uniform clothing and linen 'coatees' or round jackets for troops serving 'at the Southern Stations ... in lieu of one pair of Woolen Overalls' (see MAA 345, pp.9, 43, and Plate A1).

The coat adopted for the artillery in 1804–05 seems to have been very much in keeping with that previously worn, with some minor concessions to current fashion, including a more cutaway breast and skirts and possibly an alteration from slashed to round cuffs. The infantry uniform, finally selected from three patterns submitted to the Secretary during late 1803, was dramatically altered. The coatee form (which had fallen out of favor in 1796) was rejuvenated, although now in 'the prevailing stile of fashionable clothing in Philadelphia'. It retained the traditional scarlet facings, although the false lapels were now edged with a narrow welt of white cloth, as were the standing collar, cuffs (slit on the underside), shoulder straps, and diagonal or 'slashed' pocket flaps. False buttonholes of cord, red on the facings and blue on the flaps, corresponded with large pewter 'eagle' buttons, which were placed as follows: two on each side of the collar, eight per lapel, four per cuff and pocket flap. A new introduction was the half-turnback of red cloth rather than white, 'as the latter will soon become dirty', with a white-edged blue heart at its extreme point.

As the United States prepared for what appeared to be imminent war with Great Britain in 1808, the Purveyor struggled to provide clothing and equipage for the largest mobilisation of regular troops since the Quasi-War with France. Clothing for the five additional infantry regiments would be the same as established in 1804 for the two still in service, but uniforms and equipage patterns needed to be specified and developed for the re-established regiment of light dragoons, a regiment of light artillery and one of riflemen. While the Secretary of War, the Purveyor and other interested parties grappled over specific details of enlisted clothing and equipage throughout that year, enough of the general details had emerged by May to enable a circular to be published,

The stirrup-hilted sabers carried by the Regt of Light Dragoons in 1799–1801 and again in 1808–11 were inspired by the British 1788 light cavalry pattern. The upper example, with its iron-mounted leather scabbard, is from the Rose contract of 1807. The lower weapon is one of 2,000 produced under a 1798 contract with the US – the first 'official' pattern used by the US Army. (Courtesy Don Troiani Collection)

principally for the edification of the new officers and their tailors. Printed diagrams or patterns were supposed to be forwarded with the written descriptions, but there is no evidence that these were ever produced.

The light artillery coat was similar to that of the 'old' or 1st Regiment of Artillery, although skirts were to be shortened to coatee length. Light dragoons received an all-blue jacket based on that worn by English light dragoon and hussar corps, closed in front from neck to waist by hooks and eyes, with false lapels on the breast and profusely trimmed throughout by loopings of white cord, edgings of narrow white tape and a profusion of small pewter ball or 'buck-eye' buttons. Riflemen were to receive a grass green coatee, similar in overall cut to the infantry coatee, with black facings and yellow trimmings (including brass buttons marked 'RR'). The three new-styled corps were soon referred to as the 'helmet corps', as each had been authorised a specific form of leather cap, suitably trimmed and with distinctive corps plumes.

Legwear followed the same form as had been established for the infantry and foot artillery in 1802, although the light artillery's yellow-piped winter 'overalls' or pantaloons were to be made like the linen ones, e.g. without gaiter bottoms for wear with boots when mounted or with gaiters when on foot. Dragoon pantaloons were of blue for winter and white linen for summer, edged with white or blue cord respectively, but similarly without gaiter bottoms. The riflemen received yellow-edged green overalls with gaiter bottoms for winter service, and for hot weather green-dyed linen ones with buff or 'straw-coloured' fringing set in the outseam, to be worn with the coat or with a green hunting shirt similarly trimmed (for a more detailed description and illustration of this garment, see MAA 345, pp.18, 45, and Plate D1). Unlike the other troops, who wore sleeveless white woollen vests all the year round (these having standing collars, welt pockets and nine-button fronts since at least 1802), the riflemen received buff wool vests for winter and white linen ones for summer use.

While the troops of the US Army were perhaps better and more handsomely clothed than at any time in their previous service, there was still a great deal of dissatisfaction concerning the fit, quality of materials and style of the uniforms. Brigadier-General Wilkinson (although a scoundrel, who served at one time as an agent of Spain while senior general of the US Army) was an innovative officer who kept current with military developments. In 1808 he advocated the adoption of a 'close round about [jacket] to cover the Hips & strait breasted with red Cuff & Cape' rather than the current coat of cutaway form, to be worn with a visored leather cap with 'a flap occasionally to pull down, Cover the neck & tie under the Chin'. Dearborn, however, thought little of this proposed 'Seamans Jacket', and the matter was dropped for the time being.

When St Memin took this profile of Wade Hampton in 1809 he had just been promoted from colonel of the Regt of Light Dragoons to brigadier-general in the army. He is shown still dressed in his dragoon uniform, including a blue 'hussar' jacket with silver trim and edgings, and a helmet with a blue and white plume. Officers' helmets were made in a different fashion from enlisted headgear, and were trimmed with bearskin crests and leopardskin turbans. The silver chain apparently served as a chinstrap when necessary. (Courtesy National Portrait Gallery, Smithsonian Institution)

(continued on page 33)

1: Sergeant, 1st American Regt, 1784–85
2: Artilleryman, fatigue dress, 1785
3: Fifer, 1st American Regt, 1785–87

1: Private, light infantry,
  3rd Sub Legion, 1794–96
2: Private, 1st American Regt, 1788–91
3: Private, 2nd Sub Legion, 1792–93

B

1: Rifleman, 1st Sub Legion, 1794–96
2: Light Dragoon, 1792–97
3: Matross, Corps of Artillery, 1796–97

C

1: Infantryman, 1801–02
2: Light Dragoon, 1799–1801
3: Private, 1st Infantry;
   winter dress, 1801–03

D

1: Matross, Artillerists & Engineers, 1800–01
2: Officer, 1st Infantry; surtout, 1801–c.1803
3: Private, Corps of Engineers, 1807–10

E

1: Dismounted Light Dragoon, 1808–11
2: Private, Rifle Regiment, 1808–10
3: Private, Infantry, 1808–10

F

1: Sergeant, Consolidated Regiment, 1810
2: Officer, Infantry, 1806–10
3: Matross, Light Artillery Regt, 1808–11

G

1: Private, 4th Infantry, 1810-11
2: Private, late Whitney's Rifle Co, 1811
3: Matross, Regt of Artillery, 1810-11

THE ARMY ON THE EVE OF WAR, 1809–11

Probably painted some time between 1810 and 1812, this detail from a portrait of Maj Jacinth Laval shows what appears to be an undress uniform adopted by light dragoon officers (another portrait depicts Laval in full dress uniform, as worn by Wade Hampton). This all-blue jacket or coat is closed in front by hooks and eyes and trimmed on the breast with silver cording and ball buttons, arranged in the same fashion as found on the lapels of the uniform' jacket. The collar has silver cord edging and an embroidered six-point star, rather than the two silver-laced buttonholes of the full dress jacket. The popular civilian round hat was authorised for wear by off-duty officers in all corps, trimmed with a military cockade and loop as here. In the background can be seen Laval's silver- or steel-mounted saber with ivory grips, P-guard and bird's-head pommel. (Courtesy A.S.K.Brown Military Collection, Brown University)

Others were equally dissatisfied with the army's clothing and, with the change of administrations in 1809, took it upon themselves to develop prototype uniforms for possible adoption the following year. Brigadier-General Wade Hampton, commanding the Southern District, directed Maj Alexander Macomb of the Engineers to prepare pattern uniforms to be forwarded for possible consideration by the new Secretary of War, William Eustis. Macomb (who had earlier played a significant role in the design of the stylish Engineer officer and enlisted uniforms) forwarded two versions of an infantry coat, a long artillery coat, and a rifle 'suit' to the Secretary in late June, followed by pattern caps the following month. Eustis forwarded the coats and caps to various senior officers for their opinions during the remainder of the year, including BrigGen William Clark, Col William Duane of the Rifle Regiment, and Col Jonas Simond of the 6th Infantry. Duane (then serving on assignment as Adjutant General), Superintendent of Military Stores Callender Irvine (whose distaste for the current uniforms was apparently exceeded only by his dislike of the Purveyor, Tench Coxe), and John Armstrong (then serving as Minister to France) appear to have been other ringleaders in this fashion cabal.

On 11 January 1810 the Secretary of War informed the Purveyor that he would receive 'Patterns for the Uniform Coat of Infantry, Old Artillery, Light Artillery, Light Dragoons and Riflemen' conveyed by Gen Clark. They were to serve as patterns for the ensuing year's clothing contracts, with the exception of 'the Infantry Coat in which you will adopt such alterations as may be suggested by General Clark'. Pattern buttons were also submitted, bearing new devices for certain corps, those 'for the Old Artillery with R.A., for the Light Artillery, with L.A; for the Light Dragoons, with L.D; and for the Riflemen, with R. [on an eagle] only'.

After a great deal of communication, miscommunication, changes, and wrangling between the Secretary, the befuddled Purveyor and his contractors, and Irvine (whose duties also included inspection of all military clothing made under contract), by April 1810 the dust had nearly settled and the new pattern uniforms were in production. Initially, all five pattern coats had been made up with straight breasts that buttoned close to the waist. The artillery coat was to be trimmed with yellow lace, while the infantry coat had false buttonholes of white cord. However, due to a large back stock of the trimmings conforming to the previous uniform and other problems, all of the selected patterns were modified to incorporate surplus cord, lining materials, and other trimmings on hand. (The modifications and final appearance of these garments are discussed at length in MAA 345, as well as in the

This 1808 engraving of BrigGen
James Wilkinson was made from
a now unlocated profile portrait
by St Memin. It shows a single-
breasted coat or *surtout*, most
likely of blue with a buff 'flowing'
collar and edging, and gold
epaulettes bearing the single
silver star of his rank. The
undress uniform for general
officers was not officially
prescribed and was probably
made according to individual
taste. (Courtesy National Portrait
Gallery, Smithsonian Institution)

commentaries for Plates G and H
herein.)

In addition, contracts had
already been let for the 1810
clothing and many had
already been cut out or
completed according to
the earlier specifications.
In order to provide
for some uniformity
in issues, the Secretary
directed that most of
the stocks of old pattern
uniforms be delivered to
troops serving on the
Mississippi River and at
western posts until depleted,
while eastern troops received
priority in the distribution of the
new-styled coats. This practice was not religiously adhered to during
the actual packing, shipping, and issue – frequently through the
inter- cession of influential commanding officers, but just as often through
human error. At Fort Wayne, Indiana Territory, Capt James Rhea
acknowledged the arrival of clothing for his company of the 1st Infantry,
noting the inclusion of 'thirteen Coats of a new Uniform' which he
described as having 'a little piece of white Yarn in place of lace for the
button holes', and considered 'the meanest uniform I ever saw in the
Army except the levies of 1791'. This is a clear indication that the new
uniforms, although more modern in cut, were not necessarily regarded
as improvements by many of the troops who wore them.

The round hat worn by the infantry, equally unpopular in certain
quarters, had been supplanted by a visored felt cap of cylindrical (shako)
form in 1810. The prototype caps sent
by Macomb to the Secretary for
approval in 1809 were made
of leather and one had a
rain flap (as suggested by
Wilkinson in 1808). Istead
the form finally adopted
was the one worn since
1805 by the US Marine
Corps. The cockade was
affixed to the left side
near the top, and it was
bound around the
crown and leather-lined
visor or brim with black
worsted tape. A white
feather plume was mounted
in front of the cap, which was
further trimmed with 'lines' or
'band and tassels' of white worsted

Maj Alexander Macomb was not
only a talented engineer, and the
author of the army's first manual
on military justice; he also
contributed greatly to the
modernisation of uniforms
during the first decade of the
19th century. He is shown in this
1809 engraving by St Memin in
the undress coat of blue, with
black velvet collar and cuffs,
worn by most engineer officers
for their normal duties. The full
dress uniform was of the same
cut but with embroidered collar
and (before 1807) buttonholes.
For a detailed description of
Engineers uniforms see
MAA 345, pp.37-38.
(Author's collection)

Capt Clarence Mulford of the Regt of Artillerists is shown in this St Memin profile wearing the square-breasted but still lapelled coat adopted c.1806 and worn by many officers until the War of 1812; the buttons are 1802 artillery pattern. The scarlet facings are edged and the buttonholes bound with narrow gold lace. Note that only the bottom of the collar is edged. (Courtesy National Portrait Gallery, Smithsonian Institution)

or cotton cord. As with the uniform coats, however, it turned out that there were sufficient round hats still on hand or being delivered by contractors to fill the needs of most of the infantry throughout 1810.

It had been the custom to provide round hats with the wired bearskin crests to troops serving north of Virginia, while the southern troops and those on the western frontiers were expected to provide crests for their hats from local sources of supply, as the bearskin could not be stored or shipped any distance without a strong chance of insect infestation or other damage. The Secretary informed the Purveyor that it was immaterial whether the bearskin crests be provided for any of the hats that year due 'to the lateness' of the season, although most hats were still trimmed in that fashion by appearance-conscious commanders once they had been received. Others, such as the colonel of the 4th Infantry, converted their men's round hats into caps of the new fashion by cutting away the brim except in front and providing for the appropriate plumes and trimmings through pay or whiskey stoppages.

The cocked hats of the foot artillery, unchanged in form and trimmings since 1802, continued to be issued despite their now-outmoded form and the frequent complaints of the artillery officers, many of whom purchased hats of more fashionable style for their men, or altered the hats 'by cutting and constructing one hat from two of their fantail hats ... expensive to the soldier...[and not] durable.' The plumes or false feathers of red 'worsted ravellings', never popular, were sometimes replaced by real feathers of red or white, depending on the whim of the local commanding officer.

Moses Hook of the 1st Infantry sat for this miniature some time between his promotion to captain in 1805 (note his single silver right-hand epaulette) and his resignation of his commission in 1808. He wears his scarlet lapels fashionably buttoned across, rather than folded back and fastened down the center with hooks and eyes. Unlike his commanding officer Col Hunt (see p.22) he is shown without either gorget or swordbelt. As on most officers' uniforms of the period the lace or tape trim is very narrow – approximately a quarter-inch wide. (Courtesy Louisiana State University Art Gallery)

There was little change in the overall clothing and headdress of the army in 1811 from that adopted the previous year. Although small stocks of the pre-1810 uniform were still on hand, most troops received the 1810 pattern uniforms of their respective corps, although still closed at the breast with hooks and eyes rather than buttoned fronts, and with false cord buttonholes instead of lace or binding. One notable exception were the light dragoons, who had apparently succeeded in keeping their all-blue uniforms of the 1808 form despite a redesigned blue uniform faced with red, first proposed in 1810 and in production by 1811. Sufficient stocks of the felt caps were now available to enable most infantry in 1811 to appear in the new headgear without resorting to local modifications, although the foot artillery were not so fortunate – it would not be until the War of 1812 that their impractical and unpopular cocked hat would finally be replaced through official supply channels.

In 1801–11 infantry officers in some regiments were permitted to wear a plain uniform similar to that of their men when they were on command, fatigue or other service. This 1808 portrait of Col John Whiting, 4th Infantry, shows such a coat, with buttonholes of scarlet 'twist' on the lapels rather than silver lace. The straps of his silver epaulettes are mounted on red ground, and the front of his white vest is edged red. He holds the same silver-mounted hunting sword which he had carried in the War for Independence while an officer of the Massachusetts Line. A year later his successor would write to a subordinate that the price of 'lace at present is so excessively high' that he recommended the purchase of a 'very handsome' unlaced coat in its stead. (Ex-author's collection; courtesy Craig Bell Collection)

CONCLUSION

Largely ignored or forgotten by the public which it served, the fledgling United States Army protected the vast frontier and coastal boundaries of the new nation to the best of its abilities, despite its limited resources and minuscule size. Under the new constitutional government, soldiers received (on paper) a rather generous annual allowance of military clothing, although the arcane and ineffective system of supply and transport by contract led to shoddy materials and production standards, and frequently to late and muddled deliveries. The uniforms, equipment and tactical doctrine of the Federal army were but little changed from those of the War of Independence, which though perhaps adequate for constabulary service on the frontier would prove inadequate against a well-equipped modern army. Despite the efforts of Washington and Hamilton to keep up with European advances, few of the intended reforms had been implemented by the conclusion of the Quasi-War, although some of them were later accomplished during the Jefferson administration. The army was still outmoded in most of these respects in 1812, and little prepared for its impending war with Great Britain.

SELECT BIBLIOGRAPHY

Primary Sources:
Unfortunately, many of the Confederation and Federalist period records of the army were destroyed in an early fire that gutted War Department offices, while other official records and correspondence have become separated and widely scattered. As in MAA 345, *The United States Army*

Infantry officers were officially authorised white shoulderbelts with oval silver plates from 1799 to 1812, although the prescribed eagle device would evolve over time. This plate was probably made between 1805 and 1812, based on the form of the eagle, the dimensions, and method of manufacture. The small blank space left below the eagle is probably to accommodate either the officer's initials or sometimes the regimental designation – both practices continued well into the War of 1812. (Author's collection)

1812–1815, much of this book is based on the rich and varied collections of the US National Archives, including: Record Group (hereafter RG) 45, Office of Naval Records and Library; RG 77, Office of the Chief of Engineers; RG 92, Office of the Quartermaster General; RG 94, Office of the Adjutant General; RG 98, US Army Commands; RG 107, Office of the Secretary of War; RG 156, Office of the Chief of Ordnance; RG 217, Accounting Officers of the Department of the Treasury; and RG 360, Records of the Continental and Confederation Congresses. At the US Library of Congress, the papers of Alexander Hamilton and George Washington cannot be overlooked for the Quasi-War period. Finally, the rich and varied collections of the following institutions are invaluable to the student of the early US Army: the William L.Clements Library, U. of MI; The Lilley Library, Indiana U.; the Carnegie Library and the Historical Society of Western Pennsylvania, both in Pittsburgh, PA; the US Military Academy Library at West Point; the New York Historical Society; the Historical Society of Pennsylvania; the Indiana Historical Society; the Burton Collection, Detroit Public Library; and, finally, the research library of the Ohio Historical Society, whose impressive microfilm holdings and related collections dealing with the Harmar, St Clair, and Wayne campaigns have proved a fertile resource to this researcher. Space does not permit listing the museum and private collections of artifacts and artwork related to this subject, although some of the most important objects are reproduced as illustrations and credited to the appropriate institution or individual herein.

Useful Secondary Works:

Company of Military Historians, journal of, *The Military Collector & Historian* I-XLI (1949–2000) and the companion uniform plate series, *The Military Uniform in America*

Crackel, Theodore, *Mr Jefferson's Army* (New York U. Press, 1987)

Guthman, William H., *March to Massacre* (McGraw-Hill Book Co., NY, 1970)

Guthman, William H., *US Army Weapons, 1784–1791* (privately printed, 1975)

Jacobs, James Ripley, *The Beginnings of the US Army, 1783–1812* (Princeton U.Press, 1947)

Knopf, Richard C. (ed.), *Anthony Wayne: A Name in Arms* (U. of Pittsburgh Press, 1960)

Kochan, James L. & Earl J.Coates, *Don Troiani's Soldiers in America, 1754–1865* (Mechanicsburg, PA: Stackpole Books, 1998)

Kochan, James L., *The United States Army, 1812–1815* (Osprey, Men-at-Arms 345, 2000)

Kohn, Richard H., *Eagle and Sword* (The Free Press, NY, 1975)

Ward, Harry M., *The Department of War, 1781–1795* (U. of Pittsburgh Press, 1962)

Duncan Lamont Clinch of the 3rd Infantry probably sat for this portrait shortly after his promotion to captain in December 1810. Although some officers, such as those in the Consolidated Regiment, attempted to acquire uniforms that resembled the new 1810 enlisted coats, it is likely that most retained the long, lapelled coat seen here until 1812. The use of a 'Chapeau bras, with a white plain feather 14 inches long' is first mentioned in 1808; the hat tucked under Clinch's arm has non-regulation silver binding. (Courtesy Fort Clinch State Park, Fernandina Beach, FL; author's photograph)

Anna and Eliza Leslie were paid 75 dollars on 8 November 1809 for embroidering the device on this standard of 'The first Regiment of Light Artillery.' The ground is blue and measures two yards in the hoist by two and a half yards in the fly. (Courtesy US Military Academy Museum, West Point)

The first Regiment of Light Artillery.

THE PLATES

A1: Sergeant, 1st American Regiment, 1784–85

Handsomely clothed and accoutred, this veteran non-commissioned officer is wearing a uniform drawn from stocks on hand at the close of the War for Independence. After a few weeks of marching and fatigue duty on the frontier his appearance would be much altered. The cocked hat, trimmed with white binding and cord loopings, bears a 'Union' cockade of white ribbon or cloth over black – introduced in 1780 but still worn in the 1st American Regt as late as 1785. Accoutrements are also wartime surplus, the cartridge box being one of the 'new constructed' form copied from a British model and widely used by the Continental Army during 1778–83. His musket is a French Model 1766, on which the first US-produced longarm, the Model 1795, was based.

Two white worsted epaulettes denote his rank; that of a corporal would be marked by a single epaulette on the right shoulder. On his left sleeve can be seen a chevron of scarlet tape, another vestigial device of wartime vintage. While Harmar officially decreed in June 1787 that 'Old Soldiers who have served during the late War are to have Badges of Distinction on their left arm, one Badge for every three years service', there is evidence of this practice in the regiment much earlier. The 'badge of merit' was originally instituted in the Continental Army in 1782 by Gen Washington to recognise honorable and faithful service: one chevron for three years and two for six years. Many former Continental soldiers, displaced in post-war American society or enamored of a soldier's life, re-enlisted in the infant United States Army, and these badges continued in use for at least another decade.

A2: Artilleryman in fatigue dress, 1785

The cloth used for many late and post-war coats was of indifferent quality at best, and soon became ragged from the rigors of duty on the frontier. When Harmar marched the first troops westward in 1784 they wore hunting shirts drawn from wartime stocks to save their clothing, but these supplies soon ran out. During his company's march to Fort Pitt in 1785, Capt Doughty of the artillery purchased materials for fatigue jackets or 'roundabouts' for daily duties and fatigues, in order to save his mens' coats for parades and guard duty. Faced with scarlet at the 'cape', closed with brass buttons, and lined with scarlet baize, it proved a warm and serviceable garment. Harmar tried to have it adopted throughout the 1st American Regt (presumably with white linings for infantry), but supplies were always insufficient to the demand and many companies went without. It is known that in 1791 the 2nd Infantry (and very likely the 1st) wore similar jackets of undyed linen for hot weather service.

Hunting shirts, when available, were temporarily issued from stores for 'fatigue during the time of Hut[t]ing, & fortifying' during Wayne's command of the Legion; he wanted sufficient for all the infantry – there ever ought to be in all Armies a kind of fatigue dress...'. Only rifle troops in the Legion drew the hunting shirt as part of their regular clothing, and it would be 1802 before fatigue frocks or roundabout jackets would become part of a soldier's annual issue. A large handkerchief wrapped around the head was a common and readily contrived form of headdress, especially on the frontier, in lieu of a forage cap (the first mention of which among US troops occurs in 1801).

One of the two original artillery companies had originally been armed with short fusils, but these were replaced with French muskets and the fusils given to company-grade infantry officers 'as Fuzees are much better weapons for the Officers on the frontier than Spontoons'.

A3: Fifer, 1st American Regiment, 1785–87

As wartime stocks of clothing dwindled, the Board of Treasury let their first contract for uniforms in 1785. Included in a later amendment were special uniforms for the 'music', made up in traditional 'reversed' colors to that worn by the rest of the regiment. Included in the materials breakdown was blue serge to fully line the coat; and 20 yards of binding, sufficient to bind the buttonholes, cover the long seams and provide chevrons to the sleeves in a fashion borrowed from the British and other European armies. There is no mention of the binding on musicians' coats in the 1787 uniform regulations, and it may have been dropped at that time to save the additional expense. Winter overalls were white or blue (to the dismay of the regiment's commander), while waistcoats were of white cloth. The fifer wears a whitened buff leather swordbelt, supporting a captured 'Hessian' hanger in its brown leather scabbard (drawn from the West Point arsenal); his newly made tinned iron fife case on a sling of the same material has not yet been japanned or painted – this was possibly done later in some now-unknown regimental style. The cocked hat sports the tooled leather cockade first adopted by the regiment in 1785. His hair is worn plaited and tucked up under the hat, a practice known to have been employed during at least 1786–87; this was probably derived from the British Army, whose flank companies originally wore their hair in this fashion with their distinctive caps, and later continued the practice even as caps fell out of favor.

B1: Private, light infantry, 3rd Sub Legion, 1794–96

This soldier is marching at the 'trail arms' position in which the Legion advanced through the open woods – strewn with trees felled earlier by a tornado – during the decisive Battle of Fallen Timbers. He wears a 'round hat' with bearskin crest or roach, officially introduced in 1794 to replace the unpopular caps worn earlier by the foot soldiers. In order to build esprit de corps and aid in recognition, each Sub Legion in the Legion of the United States was assigned color distinctions for its headgear; those of the 3rd were yellow binding with yellow feathers. The vest was now cut 'round' rather than with skirts and had welted pockets instead of flaps, resulting in substantial savings in materials. Gone also was the full-skirted coat, replaced instead during 1792–93 with a coatee of similar cut, but with 'slashed' or diagonal pocket flaps rather than 'cross' pockets. This form of light infantry dress was worn by all Legion infantry (all of whom were trained to act in that role) from c.1793 until 1797.

Wayne created special light infantry companies in each of the Sub Legions in August 1793, formed from among the better marksmen and more agile soldiers, and armed with 'improved' muskets capable of an increased rate of fire. The improvement consisted 'of an alteration in the touch hole, ie by filling up the old, and drilling a new one, pretty large in an Oblique, in place of a right angular direction ... which with

39

a very fine grained powder, will most certainly preclude the necessity of priming, the concussion of the air, in forcing down the charge, will cause each Musket to prime itself; the eye of the soldier will therefore be constantly upon his Enemy, and he can pursue & load in full trot without danger of loosing any part of his powder...'.

Wayne also instituted a special cartridge for use with this arm, made with buckshot and fine-grain powder, to further expedite the loading process and to achieve some degree of effective fire in a running action against a fast-moving or hidden foe. This man's 'belly box' carries 24 rounds and is supported by a suspension strap around the neck as well as a waist belt. Those contracted in 1794 had tin 'pipes' or holes bored so shallow as to 'scarcely contain a Cartridge made of a single ball ... a Cartridge that I never did, nor never will use in Action', according to Wayne; he noted that the 'general Cartridge for actual service will be composed of One ball & three heavy buck shot...'. The defective boxes were modified or replaced, and bayonet belts and scabbards were discarded as needless encumbrances; bayonets were to be kept permanently fixed to the muskets, with fines levied should a soldier happen to lose his 'cold steel'.

B2: Private, 1st American Regiment, 1788–91
Josiah Harmar found the hats furnished by contract too small in the brim to admit a handsome cock, and too shoddy in materials to readily hold up. He had his men remove the tape binding from the hats, which were trimmed instead with a bearskin crest and a red-dyed 'buck' or deer's-tail plume; the oily nature of both fur embellishments resisted water damage and contributed to the preservation of the cheap headgear. This private's uniform coat, vest and overalls conform to the 1787 regulations. His crossbelts are of whitened buff leather; some of the companies of the 1st American Regt (1st Infantry, from 1791) were still using black crossbelts in 1791, which the commanding officer replaced by requisitioning the buff leather belts issued to many of the Levies. The knapsack is covered with bearskin, first issued in 1784 and retained in use by the regiment through at least 1791. Despite being faced with sporadic and inadequate issues of clothing, the officers of the 1st strove to maintain a smart, uniform appearance among their men when within their means.

B3: Private, 2nd Sub Legion, 1792–93
Formed from the surviving remnants of the 2nd Infantry, soldiers of the 2nd Sub Legion were to have distinctive hat trimmings of red binding and plumes. However, Wayne ordered the miserable hats converted into caps in 1792 by cutting them down and adding a front 'plate' from the

trimmings, with the further embellishment of a 'comb' of white hair collected from the tails of slaughtered cattle. This private's cap is shown without the feather, which was normally reserved for parades and guard details.

Until their new Legion clothing arrived the soldiers' old regimentals were patched and refurbished, probably achieved in at least some cases by docking the skirts, a technique Wayne had earlier employed among his troops during the War for Independence. This man's musket is French, while his cartridge box is one of 'new constructed fashion, with block bored to accommodate 29 cartridges and capable (by storing the remainder underneath the block) of carrying a full combat load of 40 rounds.

C1: Rifleman, 1st Sub Legion, 1794–96
Each Sub Legion was authorised one rifle battalion in addition to two infantry battalions, the former being furnished with rifles made by various Pennsylvania gunsmiths under 1792 contracts let by the War Department. Even before this time the 1st American Regt had armed a detachment of its best marksmen with this arm, of proven value in frontier warfare. Based on his previous wartime experience, Wayne believed 'Musquets and Bayonets the most formidable Weapon, Rifles being only Useful in hands of real Riflemen long accustomed to the use of that slow-loading yet deadly arm. To partly remedy another deficiency of the rifle – the inability to mount a bayonet – folding spears with slings were issued to the riflemen (a practice first instituted by Washington during 1777); these could be unfolded and locked to make short pikes when necessary. Shot pouches with 'hair flaps, powder horns, tomahawks and scalping knives completed the equipage of the riflemen. When the

The standard of the Legion was to have been a silver eagle on a staff, inspired – as was the legionary concept itself – by those of Imperial Rome. Each Sub Legion initially received a blue silk standard, altered from those originally made for the 1st and 2nd Infantry and the 1st and 2nd Levies in 1791. However, new standards were procured late in 1795, made in the distinguishing colors of the 1st to 4th Sub Legions – respectively white, red, yellow and green. This surviving color of the 3rd Bn, 1st Sub Legion has a white ground bearing a red shield and scroll, both edged gold, surmounted by a knotted green ribbon motif. Note the fringe on the fly (left) and the sleeve for the staff (right). (Courtesy US Military Academy Museum, West Point)

understrength Legion was reorganised in August 1793 all companies were levelled, and only three rifle companies composed of 'the most expert riflemen' were retained per rifle battalion; the other companies were armed with muskets and bayonets and annexed to infantry battalions.

The distinctive rifle uniforms are first described in the 1787 regulations: *'Hats round, white band and loop, a slip of bears skin to run across the crown. Coat blue, short, round skirt, the lapells, cuffs and cape the same with the cavalry and in addition scarlet wings on the shoulder and a margin of scarlet the width of the lapell [two inches], to be continued from the termination of the lower part of the lapells round the skirts of the coat, a scarlet rose on the hips, in which three scarlet cords, leading from the bottom, will unite, white buttons and linings, waistcoats white, no flaps, but a belt at the lower part.*

This conjectural reconstruction of the rifle coat is drawn on the above and other period military garments that seem in keeping with this description, especially the shell and jacket combination worn by British light dragoons during the same period. The lapels may have had hooks and eyes placed down their entire length, enabling the jacket to be fully closed in front, or worn in the traditional open or cutaway manner at other times, since a 'belted' waistcoat or vest was provided underneath. The rose knot and cord arrangement is one clearly found on British dragoon shells, which had extremely short skirts with 'false plaits' (sic), from which I have derived the cut illustrated. Surplus rifle coats were later used as the first uniform of the Marine Corps (with a change of buttons) when it was established, described in the 1797 Navy regulations as jackets with 'red belts', further strengthening my interpretation of both the short skirts and the belt-like configuration of the 'margin of cloth'. Hunting shirts were frequently worn in lieu of the coats during warm weather campaigning.

Note the 'clubbed' hair, the normal military fashion employed in the army until 1801, when the long hair of officers and men was officially ordered to be 'cropped' and worn short thereafter.

C2: Light Dragoon, 1792–97
As with the rifle uniforms, the dress of the light dragoons appears to have been that first prescribed in the 1787 regulations: a short coat with round skirts and no turnbacks, lapelled and faced with scarlet, with white buttons and lining. A leather 'jockey cap' with bearskin crest was the regulation headdress; this reconstruction is based on a form commonly used by the Continental Army and known to be still in store and issued out to the Legion, with three rows of (supposedly protective) chains around the crown and a turban of soft leather rather than cloth. Although a troop was nominally attached to each Sub Legion they were actually formed as a squadron and used in a more independent fashion. It is uncertain whether the dragoon caps of each troop sported the plume of its respective Sub Legion or whether a single color was adopted for all the dragoons, although the former is more likely. However, the plumes were rarely worn for daily duties, instead being reserved for parades, guard escorts and other special occasions.

Cavalry arms and accoutrements, including sabers, pistols and carbines, were drawn from stocks left over from the War for Independence; we have shown this trooper's principal arm to be a saber of 'Potter's make', one of the more popular forms in use during the late conflict.

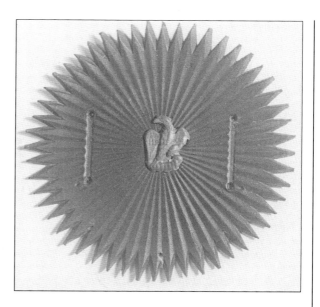

Stamped leather hat cockades were first authorised in 1785, although not officially described until 1787, when they were specified to be 4ins in diameter. In 1799 the same cockade was again prescribed, although now to be made with 'white Eagles, in the center' – those of enlisted men to be of 'tin' for all branches. As actually contracted, however, infantry eagles were made of pewter, and those for the artillery of brass as on this cockade of c.1802 found at Fort Mackinac, Michigan. (Courtesy Mackinac Island State Park Commission)

C3: Matross, Corps of Artillery, 1796–97
American artillerists had uniforms in the colors almost universally adopted by that tradition-bound branch – blue coats with scarlet facings. With yellow metal buttons and long skirts lined with scarlet, the 1784 artillery uniforms were nearly identical to those worn by the Continental Artillery from 1780 to 1783; indeed, most of the first-issue coats were of wartime vintage or pattern. Although some alteration of cut was instituted in 1787, including the introduction of standing collars, the coats worn by Legion artillerists seem to have been little changed, although short skirts began to replace long ones from 1792. As with the light dragoons, the 'paper' assignment of an artillery company to each Sub Legion was not necessarily practiced in reality. The Legion artillery, under their field commander Maj Henry Burbeck, maintained an appearance distinct from the rest of the Legion foot troops. Eschewing the colored cap and hat trimmings ordered for each Sub Legion, Burbeck seems to have preserved the traditional yellow hat binding of the artillerist, although now worn on a round hat with a bearskin crest (at least by 1794), leather cockade, and red plume.

By late 1795, with the creation of the Corps of Artillerists and Engineers, many of the artillery detachments began receiving the reinstituted long coats (the new-raised troops then being organised at West Point being the first), although it would not be until late 1796 that the issue and use of short coats ceased. Sergeants received buff leather swordbelts and yellow silk epaulettes, while corporals received

The brass 'US LD' letters made for dragoon caps beginning in 1808 were 1½ins high, as were the equivalent for the Light Artillery, although those of the Rifle Regt were a quarter-inch smaller. They were attached to the cap front plates by 'good pliable brass tongues to bend and clinch', one of which is visible here in the bend of the letter U. (Courtesy Don Troiani Collection)

epaulettes of yellow worsted. The new pattern leather artillery 'helmets' were trimmed with bearskin crests, red feather plumes, and leather cockades, and in 'point of appearance' – according to Secretary of War Pickering, who had authorised their purchase – were 'vastly to be preferred to hats'. However, 'As to Caps I never wish to see any at this place nor no other', wrote Maj Henry Burbeck from Fort Mackinac in 1797, when he learned of their arrival at western posts, and he refused to issue them to the artillery under his command. By late 1797 they had fallen into disuse even at the eastern posts, and cocked hats once again predominated.

D1: Infantryman, 1801–02
When long coats were restored to the infantry in late 1797/1798, they were trimmed with eight yards of narrow white tape, sufficient for making bound buttonholes to correspond with the buttons on the facings. A year later the binding was disallowed on the coats – at least for the uniforms under contract for the 12 additional infantry regiments, and (although the point is not quite clear) most likely for those furnished to the four original regiments. The surplus clothing made up for the additional infantry regiments (discharged in May 1800) would be worn by the remaining troops until stocks were depleted. With the exception of unlaced facings, a cockade eagle (first issued in 1799), and a white deer's-tail plume (authorised for all infantry regiments in 1801), this soldier's uniform and equipment are virtually unchanged from those worn in 1797.

D2: Light Dragoon, 1799–1801
Through the impatience of a frustrated tailor-contractor, who went ahead and made up new pattern coats before they were officially sanctioned by the dithering authorities, the light dragoons were the first of only two corps to receive the army uniforms redesigned during 1799. The coat was green, faced and lapelled with black, 'each Lappel having seven buttons', while the cuffs were 'indented at the upper part having three blind button holes double and forming an angle with one button at the point, and one at each extremity of the sides'. Shoulder straps were edged with black, and the skirts were trimmed in a similar manner to the cuffs, with three herringbone or chevron-shaped 'blind' buttonholes. Binding

was yellow, to conform to the color of the button metal, those of the officers to be of gold vellum. The lining, vest and breeches were white, the latter to be made of 'white leather'. Although helmets of a new form were specified they were never made up, sufficient quantities of the old bearskin-crested model still being on hand. Presumably the new 'ribband or sach [sic] of narrow green' was procured and attached to the old caps. The dragoons were intended to function as light cavalry and the carbine had long ago been put into store; each trooper was armed instead with the newly procured Starr pattern saber of 1798, and a pair of horse pistols saddle-mounted in black leather holsters with bearskin 'caps' or covers.

By mid-1801 the two troops of dragoons still on the establishment were ordered to be dismounted, clothed and armed to act as infantry, in which capacity they served until discharged the following year.

D3: Private, 1st Infantry; winter dress, 1801–03
Colonel John F.Hamtramck of the 1st Infantry first issued a set of standing orders to govern the order and discipline of his regiment, including its uniforms and dress, in October 1801. The section dealing with uniforms was largely based on the 'final' draft regulation of 19 December 1799, with supplemental changes introduced by the new Secretary of War and the colonel (drawing upon his extensive military experience). With most of his regiment stationed at Detroit and other northern posts, Hamtramck introduced special winter uniforms to combat the bitter cold of the Great Lakes region. Enlisted men wore white blanket coats with blue collar, cuffs and cross pockets with 'flaps standing like those of a jacket' (apparently large welt pockets). Edges were bound with blue binding and breasts were closed by blue buttons. The blue stripes woven near the ends of 'point' blankets are shown placed above the hem, based on extant 18th- and 19th-century drawings of this garment and surviving examples of later 19th-century blanket coats. Also seen here are three black stripes placed along the selvedge edge in front – two twice as long as the other – signifying that this coat was made from a '2½-point' blanket; trade blankets of this sort were graded by both size and quality in a point system and distinguished in this way. This soldier wears the blue forage cap with red trim first specified in 1st Infantry standing orders in 1801–02. (This is the first mention which I can find of forage caps in surviving US Army records between 1784 and 1815 – another being one proposed for the light dragoons in c.1808.) His winter overalls of blue wool are worn over high stockings to protect his lower legs from the biting cold.

It is unknown how long these standing orders (subsequently modified and reissued in July 1802, with no changes noted in the enlisted uniforms) remained in effect, although they probably applied until at least April 1803, the month in which Col Hamtramck died and command devolved on another officer, perhaps with differing tastes.

E1: Matross, Artillerists & Engineers, 1800–01
This artillery private or 'matross' wears the new artillery uniform designed and furnished in 1799, which retained the traditional scheme of blue faced with scarlet and yellow metal buttons. The coat was of a different cut, however, with more pronounced rounding in the breast and wider facings. The shoulder straps ended in blue wings with red edgings

the pocket flaps on the skirts were placed vertically and similarly edged, and finished with three large brass buttons. The scarlet cuffs were slashed, with blue flaps edged in red and closed by three large buttons. Each lapel had nine large buttons, and a small button was apparently added to each side of the standing collar. Although attempts had been made to provide buff crossbelts to bring uniformity to the accoutrements, at least one company still wore 'old black ones [that were] disfigur'd & worn out' in 1800. Plain cocked hats, trimmed since 1797 with a white plume, leather cockade and eagle, and yellow cockade loop, were modified by the addition of yellow binding and red plumes (initially to be of dyed deers' tails, but later made from worsted 'ravellings') in April 1801. After this date yellow binding was also added to the enlisted artillery coats, and gold buttonholes and edging to those of the officers. The soldiers' coat was otherwise unchanged in form, despite complaints from some of the officers, whose own coats had cross pockets and cuffs, being modelled on the uniform prescribed in the draft 1799 regulations still in circulation.

E2: Officer, 1st Infantry; surtout, 1801–c.1803

Although the 1799 infantry clothing was never made up or issued, various versions of the 1799 'regulations' had made their way into the field and most officers had their uniforms made up to conform with the cut and insignia recommended for their branch and grade. The use of a uniform 'surtout' (essentially a tailored overcoat) by dismounted infantry officers during cold weather is first mentioned in the 1799 regulations. With some changes in cut and trimming, surtouts were actually adopted and used as early as October 1801, at least by the 'platoon' officers of the 1st Infantry. Made of blue cloth with a scarlet standing collar and half lapels (shown here buttoned across, exposing the blue undersides), it had cross pockets 'the same as the Regimental Coats' and 4in-deep blue cuffs, with a scalloped 'slit' closed with two large buttons. The surtout had two blue 'scalloped' capes, the upper one 9ins deep in back and the lower one 10ins deep. Sergeants were also authorised to wear surtouts of the

Coat worn by Lt William S.Hamilton, who served in the 3rd Infantry 1808–November 1812; in 1810 he was part of a detachment from the 3rd serving with the 'Consolidated Regiment' at Cantonment Washington. These officers petitioned to have their 'present Uniforms ... advantageously altered, both as to Appearance and Convenience', by changing the long coat to 'a short one, bearing some resemblance to that of the Private'.

Careful examination reveals that this coat was made by altering an earlier lapelled uniform to conform closely to the single-breasted coatee first issued to enlisted infantrymen in 1810. It is trimmed in the same way as the 1810 enlisted coat, although with silver lace rather than white cord and cloth edging, and is similarly closed at the breast with hooks and eyes. There is provision for a lieutenant's epaulette on the left shoulder, and the counterstrap on the right is edged with silver lace. The skirts, somewhat longer than the enlisted mens', feature false full turnbacks of scarlet rather than 'half-turnbacks' (i.e. with only the front edge turned up) as on the coatee. The lower edge of the collar was originally edged with silver lace, as was the front edge of the left breast to correspond with that on the right. (Courtesy Louisiana State Museum, author's photos)

same form, but 'of an inferior cloth', rather than the blanket coats worn by the other ranks. Field officers (being mounted) wore blue cloaks lined red, with the same collar and capes as worn on the surtout.

Our company-grade officer is shown armed with an espontoon (re-established for infantry officers by Wayne in 1792), with a staff 'six feet, and two inches' long; and a steel-mounted regimental sword with 30in blade (slightly longer for mounted officers), trimmed with a non-regulation sword knot – the established pattern, if ever received, was to be of 'red & Silver'. His cocked hat is trimmed with black silk binding and cockade, a silver tassel, and white plume. On duty, 'round' vests and pantaloons were to be white, the latter worn inside black half-boots (full boots with black tops for mounted officers), along with buckskin gloves described as 'buff' colored in 1801 and of 'whitened leather' the following year. When on duty a crimson silk sash was worn around the waist, knotted on the right side.

E3: Private, Corps of Engineers, 1807–10

In 1802 the Secretary of War gave the Chief Engineer the privilege of establishing the uniform for this new corps. The Engineers set themselves apart from the rest of the army by adopting single-breasted, closed-front coats of the current European military fashion. The coats were deep blue with black velvet collar and cuffs – a traditional color scheme employed by engineers in many armies, including those of France and Great Britain. As specified in 1804, the enlisted coats had eight artillery buttons down the breast, trimmed with false buttonholes of narrow yellow tape extending 4ins beyond the button on each side. A button and buttonhole of the same form was placed on each side of the collar, while three chevron-shaped buttonholes were to be placed on the sleeve, the lower one butted down into the indented black cuff, and similar 'herringbone' buttonholes on each skirt. When inspected in 1805 it was found that the coats were not made 'to the original pattern', the herringbone trimmings of sleeve and skirt having been omitted. Vests and legwear were the same as used in the artillery, and although special headgear was prescribed in 1803 (a cylindrical round hat with 2in-wide brim, trimmed with yellow binding and button loop, leather cockade and a black plume), artillery 'fantail' hats and red plumes were issued through 1805. In 1807 the Engineers' round hat was made with a 'yeoman' crown – tapering in width, wider at the top than the bottom; the yellow binding was replaced with black, and black feathers replaced worsted plumes. In 1810 cylindrical felt (shako) caps of the form just approved for the infantry were issued to the engineer troops, but were rejected by the Chief of Engineers – presumably round hats continued in use until the War of 1812.

F1: Dismounted Light Dragoon, 1808–11

Due to a parsimonious President and Congress and a waning likelihood of war, very few of the light dragoons raised in

1808 ever served on horseback. Instead they were armed and accoutred as foot troops, serving in a light infantry capacity until the need for mounted troops might arise. The all-blue 'hussar' jacket had lapels framed with narrow white tape, with white cord forming a zigzag pattern between two rows of ball buttons. The collar was similarly edged and trimmed, while the breast was closed by hooks and eyes. His horsehair-crested helmet, the crown trimmed with brass reinforcing strips and identifying letters, is based on the original front plate pattern, period descriptions and excavated helmet fittings, along with an extant cap believed to have been of this pattern (illustrated on p.34, MAA 345). Its turban was to have been leopardskin, but the scarcity and expense of that fur led to bearskin being substituted in 1808 (although there is evidence to suggest that false leopardskin made of painted cloth may have been used in subsequent years). He is armed with a Model 1795 musket; his cartridge box and crossbelts are of the form first approved in 1807 and now known as 'Model 1808' accoutrements – the original contract belts were made of blackened harness leather, as shown here.

F2: Private, Rifle Regiment, 1808–10

The rifle company of Capt Benjamin Forsyth were described in May 1809 wearing 'handsome' summer uniforms of 'green coats, faced and turned up with brown [once black – a major problem with early 19th-century dyes, especially green and black, was a lack of color fastness] and yellow; green pantaloons, fringed; white vests; leather caps, high in front, on which were in large characters, U.S.R.R. with tall nodding black plumes'. The form of the rifle cap is a conjectural reconstruction based on various contemporary descriptions and archeological fragments. It had an upright front plate bearing brass initials 'US RR' for 'United States Rifle Regiment' and an inch-wide band of brass at its base. The bearskin crest over the low crown of jacked leather is based on a recommendation to replace the wire of the cap with whalebone strips – suggesting that it had a wired crest of bearskin like the infantry's round hat. The rather simple coatee of grass green cloth had black facings edged with yellow binding, with false buttonholes of cord and black-edged shoulder straps. He is armed with a Model 1803 rifle and would also carry a scalping knife and hatchet suspended

In overall dimensions, form and trimming this beaver cocked hat closely matches those described for officers of the 1st Infantry in 1802. However, the eagle in the center of the cockade is gold rather than silver, and of a form which became popular a few years later. Near-bicorn in its form, the hat was probably used by an artillery or staff officer between 1804 and 1808. (Courtesy Don Troiani Collection)

In place of the shoddily made 'US LA' cap letters worn by enlisted men of the Regt of Light Artillery, this excavated crest of gilded brass suggests that at least some officers opted for a different cap device. (Courtesy Don Troiani Collection)

from his 3in-wide waistbelt, which also mounts a 'pocket' of green-painted linen in front.

F3: Private, Infantry, 1808–10
With the exception of the new pattern accoutrements introduced in 1808, this soldier wears a uniform little changed since its first issue to the 1st and 2nd Infantry in 1804. The scarlet facings are edged with white cloth, as are the shoulder straps and pocket flaps; all the large-sized regimental buttons are trimmed with mock buttonholes of cord, with the exception of those on the hips and skirt pleats. The lapels and pockets are 'false', e.g. non-functional, as is the half-turnback of red, decorated with a white-edged blue heart. This relatively smart yet simple uniform had its share of admirers and detractors, although it was the quality of materials and finish rather than the cut (with the exception of the overalls) which was the principal cause for complaint.

G1: Sergeant, Consolidated Regiment, 1810
Detachments from the 3rd, 5th and 7th Infantry Regiments, stationed on the Mississippi River at Cantonment Washington, were formed into a 'Consolidated Regiment' in January 1810; and great effort was devoted to melding the disparate elements into a corps uniform in both drill and attire. Although issued coats of the 1804 pattern in 1810, their commanding officer was determined to convert these to a more contemporary fashion, based on the new infantry uniform approved that year. Using a pattern coat of the 1810 form which was to hand that summer, the lapelled coats were recut and made up into single-breasted ones by the company tailors. Breasts were only 11–12ins long depending on the soldier's size, which still allowed the bottom of the vests to be seen underneath. Lace was disallowed on the uniforms of the privates, with the exception of senior musicians. Sergeants' coats were to be fully laced, while those of corporals were laced only on the collar and cuffs; we read that a 'large majority of the Sergeants ... [petitioned and received] permission to put Silver cord and plated buttons on their Coats' in lieu of white lace and pewter buttons. Besides the plated buttons and silver cord holes on his fully trimmed coat, our sergeant's rank is readily apparent by the worsted epaulettes worn on both shoulders (corporals having but one on the right shoulder). From c.1800 the epaulettes of infantry NCOs were red, while the artillery still wore yellow.

There being insufficient winter overalls for all the men in one color, non-commissioned officers drew the white ones first, after which the troops were ordered to exchange their overalls with one another 'so that a company shall be all blue or all white'. White linen summer overalls were ordered always to be worn tucked inside blackened gaiters.

The use of bayonet belts had first been prohibited in 1793 and this practice continued among most of the troops, especially those at the western and southern stations, for many years. Thousands of muskets had their bayonets permanently brazed to the muzzles in 1802, and while we do not know if arms of this form were used at Cantonment Washington, the garrison still wore their bayonets always fixed in 1810. Cartridge boxes in use during 1799–1808 included the 'belly box' form as well as the 'British' pouch suspended by a crossbelt of white webbing or leather (either buff or harness leather, blackened or sometimes painted white). The latter form of cartridge box must have predominated at the Cantonment, as black belting was ordered to be worn with accoutrements for regular duties, and 'white crossbelts' were obtained for use on parade and guard mounts. It is doubtful that any of the new 1808 accoutrements (including bayonet belts) had found their way to this remote post by 1810, although sergeants would certainly have had belts for their swords.

Bearskin-crested hats with their normal trimmings remained the official headdress in this 'regiment', although the white feathers previously worn by many of the troops were disallowed after late October except among non-commissioned officers and the music, the remainder being required to wear the 'regulation' plumes of white deers' tails.

G2: Officer, Infantry, 1806–10
The dress of infantry officers was largely governed by varied interpretations of the incomplete and unofficial 1799 uniform regulations, supplemented (as in the case of the 1st Infantry) by regimental standing orders. By c.1806 the cut of the coat had changed from the cutaway form to a straight, though still double-breasted front. The scarlet lapels could be displayed fully and the front closed by pairs of hooks and eyes placed on the innermost edges of the lapels; or the lapels could be fashionably lapped across each other, as shown here. Narrow silver lace was used to edge and bind the false buttonholes on the facings and pocket flaps. The skirts, turned up with false white turnbacks joined at their juncture with a red cloth diamond, still reached down to the back of the knee. Underneath were worn a white vest and pantaloons, the latter tucked into black half-boots or 'Hessians' (when on foot). A 3in-wide shoulderbelt of buff leather was mounted with a silver belt plate bearing an eagle device, and supported a

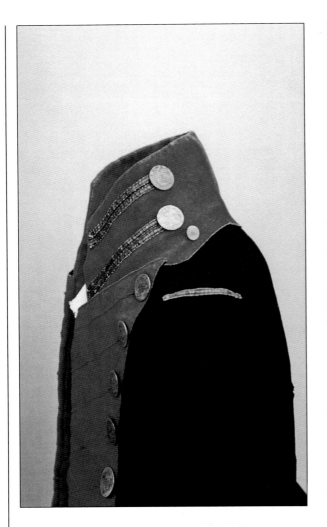

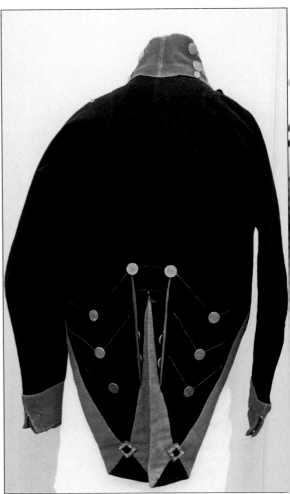

This coat belonged to Adam Larrabee, who was commissioned as a second lieutenant in the Regt of Light Artillery in 1811. Made in the fashion of c.1805–10, with a lapelled straight breast, it has on the left shoulder a gold lace strap and button for an epaulette – the proper insignia for a lieutenant. The skirts are long, rather than short as prescribed for the regiment, and are trimmed with the herringbone 'buttonholes' frequently associated with mounted troops. These details, coupled with the lack of laced holes anywhere but on the collar, suggest a regimental undress uniform. Another possibility is that Larrabee wore this coat while a cadet at the US Military Academy, 1808–11; cadets had been allowed to wear artillery uniforms, including a 'gold strap with fringe on the left shoulder', long before an official cadet dress was established. (Courtesy Iowa State Museum)

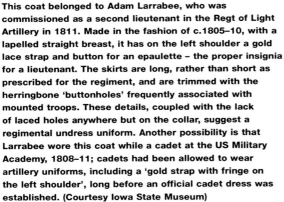

steel- or silver-mounted sword. The cocked hat had generally given way, among the more fashionable, to a *chapeau bras* with white feather plume, bound with black silk tape or silver lace. This full uniform would continue in use with little modification until at least 1810.

G3: Matross, Light Artillery Regiment, 1808–11

Horse or 'flying' artillery, although proposed during the Quasi-War, were not officially authorised until 1808 when the Light Artillery Regiment was created. Only a small portion of the regiment ever received the proper accoutrements and equipage for such service (not to mention the requisite horses); and the bulk of the regiment served as foot artillery or infantry as occasion demanded. Uniforms were similar to those worn by the 'old' Regiment of Artillery during 1804–10 although with shorter skirts (the herringbone form of the skirt trimming is conjectural and based on an extant officer's coat). Although a new straight-breasted, closed coat was approved for the regiment in 1810, few appear to have been made up and issued before 1811. It was the leather cap, with its blue and red plume and 'US LA' insignia, that was the distinguishing feature of this corps. In addition to a visor it had two vertical 'wings', the front piece being edged with a margin of bearskin. In form it appears to have been similar to British light infantry and forage caps of the 1790s–1810s, by which it was probably inspired.

H1: Private, 4th Infantry, 1810–11

One of the first corps to be issued the new infantry uniform of 1810, the 4th Infantry still received the hats of the old pattern in that year; their commanding officer ordered these to be cut and converted to approximate the form of the new felt infantry cap. To complete the caps, he directed two of his sergeants to purchase white plumes (their 'rent' for the year, in exchange for the privilege of operating a regimental sutler's establishment), and acquired 'bands' and tassels as well. For parade the 4th wore white pantaloons tucked into white gaiters, but for general duty black gaiters were worn with the summer pantaloons. Despite prohibitions in orders, many old soldiers in this regiment and others frequently cut the tongues or bottoms off their winter overalls and instead wore them with the issue summer gaiters on campaign, as seen here. According to an eyewitness who saw the 4th at the opening of the War of 1812, still dressed in the uniforms worn at the battle of Tippecanoe, the 'Colonel was permitted to uniform them to suit himself, and it was the first time I ever saw the bucket cap, with cord and tassels and the cartridge box worn around the waste, instead of over the shoulder of the coatee ...'. Although the cartridge box may have been of the 1790s belly box form, it is shown here as an 1808 pattern mounted with sliding loops to a waistbelt converted from its original sling; based on an example in the author's collection, this was the precursor of a practice commonly employed during the Civil War half a century later.

H2: Private, late Whitney's Rifle Company, 1811
Despite its tendency to fade, the grass green uniform with black facings was retained for the Rifle Regiment in 1810, although the new pattern coats had plain, straight breasts closed with hooks and eyes rather than cutaway fronts with lapels. The skirts had green linings; and black wings, with green cord edging and fringe, graced the ends of the black-edged shoulder straps. The long side seams on the backs of the coats were covered with black cord, and false buttonholes of green cord were placed on the cuffs, collar and breast. The trefoil or 'claw' ends of the holes shown here on the breast and collar are mentioned in some of the letters concerning 1810 uniforms, and their placement is partly based on an extant coat of a volunteer rifle company, believed to have been inspired by the regular army version. The continuation of the trefoil-finished cord holes in the 1814 rifle uniform (see MAA 345) also supports my conjectural reconstruction.

One company of the Rifle Regiment, 'late Whitneys' (still known by the name of its former commander, who resigned just before the Tippecanoe campaign) was attached to the 4th Infantry in 1811. The men's defective rifles were turned in for repair and they were armed and accoutred as infantry during the campaign. Considering the nature of their service it is most likely that the troops retained their tomahawks and knives, which were mounted in sliding 'cases' attached to the waistbelts. The 1808 leather cap remained in use among the Rifles until replaced in 1812.

Although worn by a member of a volunteer rifle company, this grass green coatee was probably copied from that adopted for the US Rifle Regt in 1810. Closed down the front with hooks and eyes, it has false buttonholes made of cord finished at the inner ends in 'claws' or trefoils – cf Plate H2. (Courtesy US Military Academy Museum, West Point; author's photo)

H3: Matross, Regiment of Artillery, 1810–11
The 'old artillery' were to have received a new coat decorated on its breast with three rows of 'RA' buttons, the middle row to button closed, connected by false buttonholes of yellow binding. Instead, during 1810–11, as on the new coats of the other corps, the central row of buttons was replaced with hooks and eyes down the single-breasted front. The coat's mock buttonholes were made of yellow cord rather than lace, although the collar, breast edges, pocket flaps, and turnbacks were still edged with yellow binding. Its skirts were long, almost reaching to the knee, lined and faced with scarlet to match the facings. Vest and overalls were unchanged, as was the cocked or 'fantail' hat shown at the feet of this off-duty soldier; its plume of red worsted, reserved for parade and other duties, has been removed. It was a long-standing custom in many armies for soldiers leaving the garrison in uniform to wear their sidearms, in this case bayonet and shoulder belt – a practice falling from favor due to wounds received in dram-shop altercations.

INDEX

Figures in **bold** refer to illustrations

1st American Regiment **A1**, **A3**, **B2**, 3, 8, 12, 39, 40

Armstrong, John 33
artillery
    1784-95 **A2**, 11, **12**, 15, 39
    1796-1800 **C3**, **E1**, **16**, 19, **19**, 41-42, 42-43
    1801-08 **20**, 21, 23, 24, **35**, **46**
    1809-11 **G3**, **H3**, 33, 35, 36, 46, 47

belt plates **18**, **37**
buttons 19, 33

'*Chesapeake-Leopard* Affair' 6
chronology 3-7
Clark, Brigadier-General William 33
clothing contracts 9, 34
coats
    1784-91 8, 9, 11
    1792-96 **11**, 13, 14, **14**, 15, 41
    1797-1800 **13**, 16, **16**, 19, **19**
    1801-08 **20**, 21, **21**, 22, **22**, 23, 24, **35**, 42, 42-43, **46**
    1809-11 33, **38**, **43**, **47**
cockades 8-9, 11, 18, 19, 34, **41**
Consolidated Regiment, the **G1**, 45
Continental Army, the 3, 7, 8

Darke, Lieutenant Colonel William **5**
Dearborn, Henry, Secretary of War 21, 22, 22-23, 24
dragoons **C2**, **D2**, **F1**, 7, **13**, **15**, 16, 19, 24, **24**, **33**, 36, 41, 42, 44
Duane, Colonel William 33

engineers **E3**, 5, 6, **34**, 44
establishment 3, 4, 5, 6, 6-7, 23
Eustis, William, Secretary of War 33
exercise **20**

Fallen Timbers, battle of, 20 August 1794 5, 39
fashion, influence of 10
Fish, Major Nicholas 9

Great Britain 6, 7, 23
Greenville, Treaty of, 1795 5

Hampton, Brigadier-General Wade **24**, 33
Hamtramck, Colonel John F. 42
Harmar, Lieutenant Colonel Josiah **3**, 4, 8, 11, 12, 39, 40
Harrison, William Henry 7
hats
    1784-91 8, 9, 11, 12
    1792-96 **10**, 14, 15, 40
    1797-1800 18, 42
    1801-08 21, 24, **42**, 43, 44, **44**
    1809-11 **24**, 34-35, 36, **38**, 44, 45, 46
Indians 4, 5, **5**, 7
infantry **D1**, **D3**, **F3**, **H1**, 7, 11, 19, 21, 23, 33, 42, 45, 46-47
Irvine, Callender 33

Jefferson administration, the 21, 22

Knox, General George, Secretary of War 7, 8, 11-12, 13, 14

Legion of the United States, the **B1**, **B3**, **C1**, 5, **10**, 13-15, 39, 39-40, **40**, 40-41
Levies 4, **5**, 12-13
Louisiana Purchase, the 6

Macomb, Major Alexander 33, **34**
Massachusetts, revolt in 1786 3
McHenry, James, Secretary of War 18, 19, 20
military academy 6, **8**, 22
Mississippi River 6
musicians **A3**, 9, 39

non-commissioned officers **A1**, **G1**, 9, 39, 45
Northwest Ordinance, the, 1787 3

officers
    1784-91 **4**, **5**
    1792-96 **7**, **9**, **10**, **11**, 14, **14**
    1797-1800 15
    1801-08 **E2**, **21**, **22**, **35**, **36**, 43-44, **46**

1809-11 **G2**, **24**, **33**, **34**, **37**, **38**, **43**, 45-46

Pike, Major Zebulon **22**
Pinckney, Major General Charles Cotesworth 18
Pratt, Captain John **4**
Purveyor of Public Supplies, the 20, 21, 21-22, 33

rank, insignia of 10, 39
riflemen **C1**, **F2**, **H2**, 5, 7, 24, 39, 40-41, 41, 44-45, **47**
role 36

Spain 6
St Clair, Major General Arthur 4
standards **38**, **40**
supply system 36
surtout **E2**, **34**, 43-44

Tippecanoe, battle of, 7 November 1811 7
Treasury, Board of 9, 39

uniforms 36
    1784-96 7, **7**, 7-8, 9-10, 10-11, 12
    1797-1800 **15**, 15-16, **17**, 18-19, 19-20, 20-21
    1801-08 23, 24
    1809-11 33, 34
    fatigue **A2**, 9, 10, 23, 39
    overalls **8**, 11-12, 16, 19, 21, 24
    style 10
    winter **D3**, 42

War of 1812 (1812-14) 36
War of Independence (1775-83) 7, 36
Washington, General George 6, 7, 15, 18, 39
Wayne, Major General Anthony 5, **9**, **11**, 13, 13-14, 15, 39-40, 44
weapons
    bayonets 45
    muskets **A1**, **F1**, 39, 39-40, 44
    officers **E1**, 44
    rifles 40
    swords **23**, 41
Whiskey Insurrection, Pennsylvania **6**
Wilkinson, Brigadier General James 20, 24, **34**